LIFE AND TRADITION IN
NORTHUMBERLAND AND DURHAM

LIFE & TRADITION
in
NORTHUMBERLAND
and DURHAM

by Frank Atkinson

with a map
31 drawings in text
and 142 photographs

DALESMAN BOOKS · 1986

The Dalesman Publishing Company Ltd.,
Clapham, via Lancaster, LA2 8EB

First published by J.M. Dent & Sons Ltd., 1977
This edition 1986

Printed in Great Britain by
Fretwell & Cox Ltd.,
Goulbourne Street, Keighley, West Yorkshire

ISBN 0 85206 871 9

Contents

Photographs

Drawings

Foreword

It was once put to me that, as a Yorkshireman, I had no business to be portraying the North-East in a regional 'social history' museum, let alone writing a book about its identity! This view, I am happy to say, is not very strongly felt, but the fact that it could still be phrased—even in semi-jest—suggests that the region maintains an awareness of its isolation. At least strangers do not have stones thrown at them in the street, as is said to have been the case two centuries ago—though truthfully that happened in other parts of the country too!

What I do believe is that an 'incomer' can often observe characteristics and regional features which remain unnoticed by the resident, who has no basis on which to make comparisons. If the countryman has always used a particular shape of scythe—and never seen any other—how can he know that it is peculiar to his region?

So, over some nineteen or twenty years the North-East has been a source of enjoyment to me, and the discoveries I have made, of its scythes, its possers, its dess-beds, its coal-mines and its lead-mines, and particularly of its people, their words and their customs—all these have given me a real sense of satisfaction. I have enjoyed observing, recording and attempting to preserve something of this flavour of the region and hope this book will help to impart some of this pleasure to its readers.

As to another view of this regional unity, about the time that this book was largely completed, I came across a paper recently published in the journal *Regional Studies* entitled 'Regional Culture and Identity in Industrialized Societies: the Case of North-East England'. This is a paper based on a survey which investigated the 'sense of place and local identity' in the North-East, and in it the claim is made that although residents of the region feel that many of their links are with the area around the town in which, or near which, they live, yet they tend also to think of themselves as being North-Easterners, or even 'Geordies'. As these writers point out, although certain regional folk customs seem to be in decline, the overall strength of regional culture, expressed especially in the symbolic Geordie, is not diminishing so markedly. Indeed, they believe that the maintenance of a north-eastern cultural unity is at least in part attributable to the relative isolation from the rest of the country. These investigators found that a majority of their survey sample had not lived outside the North-East and hence this sense of isolation and unity.

The writers further suggest that there seems to be a commonly shared regional identity, resulting quite possibly from a sense of regional under-development and they go so far as to propose that, if regional government were ever to be established, one of its roles might be a positive attempt to maintain the flavour and importance of this regional culture.

All this seems to me to support, in a more quantified way (for the paper has several tables supporting its conclusions), the general theme which I hope comes through in this book: that there is a sense of regional unity in the North-East, and that there has been, and to some extent there still is, a regional culture whose origin one can in some part trace back through the region's history. Long may it survive. Howay Geordie!

Foreword to Second Edition

In the nine years which have followed the first edition of this book Beamish has gone from strength to strength and its visitors, now totalling several millions, have continued to enjoy its realism as well as the nostalgia it can arouse. Alas many of the objects mentioned in this book can now only be readily seen in this regional open air museum, for the break up of so many pit villages, urban streets and rural clusters has led to a loss of the old ways. Everyone now hankers for central heating, a telly and a video. And indeed why shouldn't they? But no longer do they sit round the fire for 'a bit crack' and talk about the olden times.

Fortunately the Beamish collections have grown as the region's houses, shops and pits have changed, so that there can scarcely be a single facet of northern life which is not now well-represented there.

Many of the experiences and recollections recorded here are still fresh in my mind though alas many of the informants are no longer there to reminisce. The North East has become a much blander place than it was when I first came here and its broad-spoken old miners with their 'pitmatic' dialect have virtually disappeared. Yet I hope that this book will continue to give pleasure and perhaps even instruction to those who still search for those now-fewer variations which continue to give this region its character and help it still to be different from other parts of England.

Acknowledgments

This book could scarcely have been written, and certainly not illustrated, without the collections of BEAMISH: North of England Open Air Museum, and indeed it may partly be taken as a kind of guide to some of those collections. The older photographs used here come almost entirely from the Beamish Photographic Archive, which itself is a tribute to the many people who have given old postcards and other photographs and negatives to the museum. Most of the recent photographs have been taken by the author. Plate 115 (Mrs Lough, quilter) is reproduced by courtesty of the Westminster Press and Plate 91 (Esh Winning from the air) is by courtesy of Professor McCord and the University of Newcastle upon Tyne. All the specimens illustrated by drawings are from the Beamish collections and have been drawn by Gill Humphrys. Fig 2 is based on a paper by Dr E. Sunderland (British Association volume for *Durham*, 1970), Fig. 14 is based on a paper by Dr Brian Roberts (*Mediaeval Archaeology*, 1972) and Fig. 28 is based on maps by Orton and Wright (*A Word Geography of England*, 1975), those maps being based on copyright material in the Institute of Dialect and Folk Life Studies, The University of Leeds. The drawing for Figure 13 is by Peter Brears. I am indebted to Mrs Common for permission to use the vivid quotations from Jack Common's auto-biographical novel *Kiddar's Luck*; and parts of Chapter 9 are based on recollections written by Mr Richard Morris. Much of the information on place-names is based on a paper by V. E. Watts in the *Durham* British Association Volume.

The many informants, some now alas dead, whose recollections make up a great part of this book are generally referred to in the text, though passing recollections are not always identified. To everyone who has helped in this way, knowingly and unknowingly, the author expresses his thanks. Recollections have been taken from records built up by Beamish and by the Northumberland County Record Office, and from correspondence linked with a BBC north-eastern television programme *The Yesterday Show*. My thanks are particularly given in this latter context to Roger Burgess, Producer of that programme.

Rosemary Allan and John Gall of the Beamish Museum have given unstinted help and without the skill and patience of Trish Hall the much be-scribbled text could never have been deciphered and typed.

The lyric from 'Close the coalhouse door' by Alex Glasgow is reproduced by permission of Robbins Music Corp. Ltd, 138–140 Charing Cross Road, London.

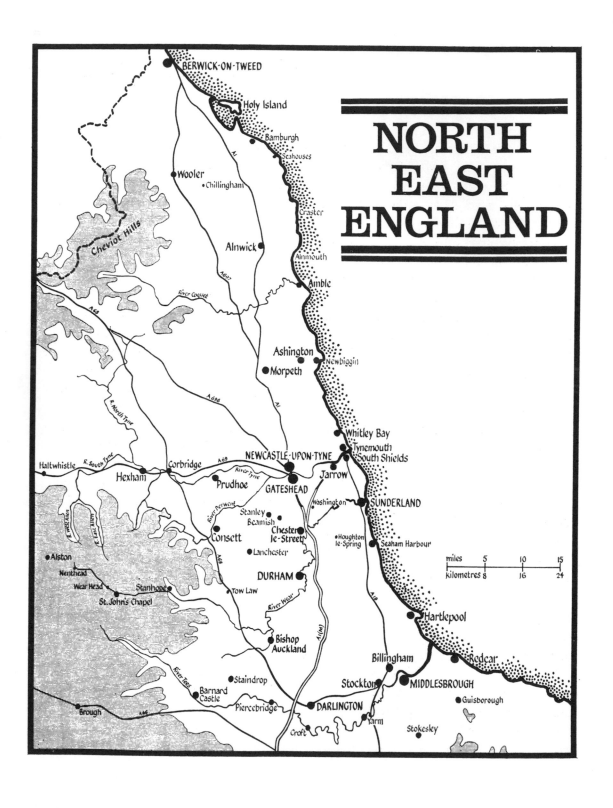

NORTH EAST ENGLAND

1 The Shape of the Land

Northumberland and Durham make up the most northern part of England and are among its least-known counties. Such ignorance, often cherished by North-Easterners since it protects many unspoilt valleys, hills and sandy beaches, is in part due to their distance from the populous midlands and southern counties, and in part to the region's own inward-looking character. This inward-lookingness is not only geographical in origin, but also characteristic of an isolated population.

In the following chapters an attempt is made to identify something of the character of the North-Easterner and to try and suggest why he is how he is, why he speaks as he does and how he has come to adopt his various beliefs and habits. To do this, it will be helpful first to look at the land in which he lives, for so much of the north-eastern way of life has been affected by the rocks and minerals, and the hills in which they lie.

North-east England is geographically somewhat isolated from the rest of England and indeed from Scotland too. To the north west lie the Cheviot Hills, along the western border are the Pennines and to the south the Cleveland Hills. Thus the east coast, far from being a barrier, has often proved the most accessible point for invaders, at several stages during the region's history. East-west access across the hills has never been easy and is in effect limited to two crossings, that of the Tyne Valley near the middle of the region, and the Stainmore Pass further to the south. This geographical isolation has, from time to time, resulted in some degree of cultural isolation and the dual effects of population intrusion from the east and isolation from the west and south are looked at in Chapter Two. These factors have had a great deal to do with the shaping of the people who inhabit north-east England.

Whilst the shape of the land has had some effect on the characteristics of the region's population, those same rock formations have also been responsible for the direction which the region's industrial development has taken. Without coal or iron the North-East would be very different: it would possibly still be the rural backwater which so much of it was up to the early years of the nineteenth century.

Certainly it would not have gained the reputation, now almost entirely unjustified, of an unwholesome, grimy and depressing environment.

The structure of the region and the origins of its mineral wealth can best be seen by taking a superficial look at its geology. In the north the Cheviot Hills represent the much-weathered remains of a large volcano and into the centre of this pile of lava has been squeezed a mass of granite. Wrapped round the south eastern flanks of these hills lie beds of sandstone, notably the Fell Sandstones. These can be traced northwards from Redesdale through Rothbury Forest to Berwick on Tweed, generally 700 to 1000 feet thick (240 to 300 metres) and producing a pronounced stepped outline on the skyline, especially when looking northwards from near Rothbury. This imposing scarp is cut through by only two rivers, the Aln and the Coquet, both of which have succeeded in breaking across it at lines of geological weakness. Being hard quartz sandstones, these rocks give rise to barren heathery moorlands, which rise in the Simonside Hills to over 1400 feet (430 metres).

If the Cheviot massif can be seen as one great pivot-point of the region's geological structure, another is the large area of limestones and associated rocks, often called the Alston block on account of the small market town lying to the west of its centre. This has been a relatively stable area, whilst geological activities have gone on around its edges. To its east lie beds of Coal Measures dipping gently to the east and these in turn have been covered to their south east by beds of Magnesian Limestone. These themselves were then partially covered by later rocks lying towards Middlesbrough and south of the Tees.

The topography of Northumberland and Durham can now be seen as two high areas: the Cheviot massif, hard rocks lying to its south and east, and the Alston block or North Pennine massif through which run Weardale and Teesdale. Between these two areas of highland runs the Tyne gap. To the east the Coal Measures, made up mostly of softer rocks, result in a gentle landscape, relieved only here and there by slight escarpments of sandstone. Across country, by contrast, run the rugged and spectacular crags of the Great Whin Sill, an igneous rock (i.e. of volcanic origin) intruded into the country rocks and stretching from the far west of our region near Haltwhistle, north-eastwards to the coast at Dunstanburgh, Bamburgh and the Farne Islands. Its thickness can vary from 20 feet to 240 feet (6 m to 74 m), though it is generally about 100 feet thick (30 m). It is also to be seen in upper Teesdale, being responsible for that fine waterfall, High Force.

All the rock formations so far mentioned are what the geologist calls 'solid geology': often of immense age and great thickness. Spread superficially over these are much later deposits left by glacial action which at one time affected the whole of the region. The 'ice-age' was not one simple stretch of time, but a complex of alternating cold and warmer periods, with sheets of ice moving, at various times and in various directions. On occasion during the ice age, glaciers crept over from Scotland and from the Lake District and left many kinds of deposits across Northumberland and Durham. One can gain some idea of the extent of their movement by the 'erratics': small and large fragments of rock originally dragged from mountainous regions by the passing ice movement and deposited towards the extremity of the glacial activities. Thus pieces of a characteristic granite from Shap (to the east of the Lake District) can be traced to the north and south of the Tyne Gap and the Stainmore Gap, indicating glacial movements along these two crossings; traces of Cheviot granite can be found down eastern Northumberland and Durham as far as the area around Stockton on Tees; and fragments of Criffel granite are found in central Northumberland (Criffel is a hill overlooking the Nith estuary about nine miles south of Dumfries).

Other traces of glaciation are of a more structural character. For example, as the glaciers began to melt, large lakes were created high above the normal drainage surface and these often found escape routes which cut across the normal drainage patterns. A very good example of such an overspill channel is the great trench to the east of Ferryhill in County Durham. This narrow gap almost 200 feet deep and only half a mile wide once drained a lake lying south of Durham and called by geographers 'Lake Wear'. Not all spillways or glacial overflow channels have been left deserted as at Ferryhill, for another channel, which was cut through the Magnesian Limestone to the east of Chester-le-Street by a glacial lake in central Durham, is now occupied by the River Wear, diverted and flowing east to Sunderland. In pre-glacial times the Wear flowed north to join the Tyne and that old route is now followed by the tiny river Team.

Northumberland also shows many signs of glacial drainage and as an example one can point to the deep channel of Shawdon dene, near Glanton, cut through the Fell Sandstone by overflow from 'Lake Glendale'. Present-day drainage by the Breamish and Till goes northwards, but the deserted channel has provided a route for both road and rail (the latter now deserted) across the Breamish-Aln watershed.

Nearby, the area to the south west of Wooler is scattered with a chaotic assortment of gravelly mounds enclosing ill-drained peaty hollows, remains left by the stagnant ice mass as it melted away. These 'kettle-moraines' are matched by other deposits of rock, clay and sand, which were often left in lines parallel to that of the edge of the receding ice and are known as 'kames'. Such mounds can be identified in many eastern parts of the counties, a notable example, the Bradford kame, lies a little distance inland from Bamburgh. At right-angles to the kames are 'esker-trains' and good examples run westwards through the Tyne Gap, indicating the direction along which the glacier retreated. Others can be seen on Cotherstone Moor, indicating the westward retreat of the ice across Stainmore.

The solid underlying rocks, as has now been shown, have been largely responsible for the grandeur of the North-East's landscape, though in many parts they are also overlain by glacial deposits. Furthermore, these solid rocks such as granites, sandstones and limestones, have not only provided fine views and dramatic building sites; they have been the source of the region's wealth. The region owes its past economic development to these rocks and their minerals, and much current development is also similarly dependant. One has only to think of North Sea oil, of coal being mined out under the North Sea, of salt being extracted south of Hartlepool, of potash being mined in the Cleveland Hills and of fluorspar being taken out of Weardale to see that the region is still partly dependant on its mineral wealth.

In the past coal has probably been the best known mineral of the region and has been of great significance in the industrial growth of the region. Coal seams in fact form only a very small proportion of great thicknesses of rocks—sandstones, shales and others—which are together called the Coal Measures, and in the Northumberland and Durham coalfield these average around 2,000 feet (615 m) in thickness. The coal seams—perhaps each averaging 3 feet thick—lie within a thickness of about 800 feet (245 m) of the Coal Measures and have been given names which echo through the recent social history of the North-East: the Brockwell seam, the Busty, Harvey, Bensham and High Main seams.

It is also interesting to note that even such a consistently distributed mineral as this (for a given seam can generally be identified from one side of the coalfield to the other) has appreciable variations in its make-up as it is traced across country. Thus the coals of West Durham, though now almost entirely worked out, were of a very good grade especially for coke production, and this was one of the reasons for the development of the steel industry at Consett. To the north and east the coal becomes slightly poorer in quality, with a higher percentage of volatile materials. Thus the coking industry of west Durham has been replaced, as one moves to the east, by gas making and the production of steam and house coal. Nowadays coal 'blending' has removed these variations and inequalities, but their past exploitation has left its mark on the landscape, particularly in the shape of ruined 'bee-hive' coke ovens in West Durham.

Limestone is possibly the most important of the bulk minerals within the region and lime kilns, of the type used for local production of lime, are found scattered round most of the limestone areas. In these kilns crushed limestone was burned to

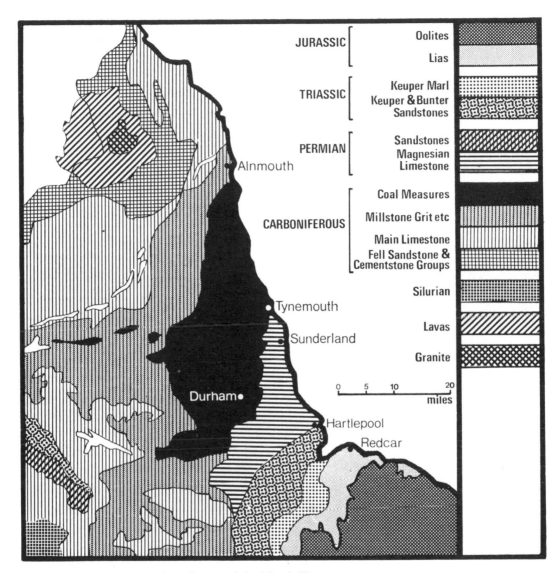

Fig. 1. *A simplified geological map of the North-East.*

'quick lime' which was used for building purposes before the advent of cement. 'Slaked lime', made by quenching or throwing water on to quick lime, was used on the land, before being replaced by the many complex and expensive materials used today by the farmer. In more modern times limestone has been quarried and burned on an enormous scale and one only has to point, in this connection, to the very large cement works now to be found in Weardale.

In East Durham a different limestone, known as Magnesian Limestone, is of great importance in the iron and steel industry. In addition to the calcium carbonate or common limestone this rock contains a high proportion of dolomite or magnesium carbonate. And dolomite is used to make refractory bricks from which furnace linings are constructed in the steel-making industry. It also has other, though less important, uses in the pharmaceutical, glassmaking and textile industries. Magnesian Limestone is worked in central east Durham in several large quarries, notably in the area between Coxhoe and Mainsforth. The life of a quarry-man or a lime-burner is now vastly different from that of last century, when this was an arduous and far from healthy occupation, as a result of mechanisation on a large scale. Fireclay, generally associated with coal seams, has been obtained from both surface and underground workings and used for the manufacture of re-fractory goods and sanitary ware. This has been a long established industry, though now much more concentrated than originally. Brick clays occur widely throughout the region including Coal Measure shales such as are worked at Lumley and Pelaw in Durham and Ashington and Throckley in Northumberland. Other clays cover large areas of east Durham and Northumberland and are also widely used for brick making. Newcastle and Sunderland were largely built of bricks made from this.

Natural building stone, although now largely superseded by other materials, is still used for such things as kerbs, flags and for ornamental purposes. Good sandstones are found throughout the Coal Measures and the older parts of towns in the coalfield are generally built of sandstone derived from small local quarries, while in east Durham Magnesian Limestone, producing a rather soft and not very durable yellowish stone, can be seen in many older buildings, now unhappily often rather badly weathered. The Whin Sill, that very hard igneous rock which has been responsible for several natural dramatic features such as High Force, the sites of Bamburgh and Dunstanburgh Castles, and the outcrops along which the Roman Wall has been built, has been used as a roadstone, both as blocks or setts and as a crushed grit.

In the centre of the Alston massif metal mining has gone on for many centuries. The minerals mined here last century, such as lead and zinc, have now been largely replaced by the mining of fluorspar which is required as a flux in steel making and for the manufacture of fluorine compounds. Thus a mineral which for long was regarded as waste, and tipped accordingly, is now being mined, often by the re-opening of deserted leadmines.

Another mineral now no longer worked in the north east is iron-ore, once the basis of the early iron industry. Of the many iron works present last century, such as those near Bellingham, Redesdale, Wylam, Walker, Jarrow, Consett, Tow Law,

Witton Park, Stanhope, Birtley, Tudhoe and Ferryhill, only Consett is left as the
sole inland working site. Even recollections of most of these works and their
associated skills have been lost, and little can be seen apart from a few ruined
buildings such as a massive engine house at Ridsdale in Northumberland and
terraces of workers' houses at Tudhoe.

From all this it will be seen that the heavy industries of the North-East, coal,
iron, lead and limestone, traditionally those on which the original prosperity of the
region was based, stem from the mineral content of the landscape. The continuing
theme of the effects of these minerals will be seen throughout this book, for their
extraction, their preparation and their uses have controlled not only the development of the land, but its subsequent settlement patterns and its very traditions and
the way of life of its people. 'To take coals to Newcastle', the well-known phrase
indicating something entirely unnecessary, points to the part which coal has
played in the history of the region.

Two other heavy industries notable in the region's history, shipbuilding and
mechanical engineering, have so far not been mentioned. These have been in-
directly derived from the coal and iron industries, for coal was mined mostly for
export and this led to land transport and shipping developments which themselves
sponsored ship-building and railway systems, and engineering not unnaturally
followed.

The horse-drawn colliery wagonways of the eighteenth and early nineteenth
centuries came to be known as 'Newcastle roads' and one can hardly be surprised
that the world's first public railway system began in County Durham. The
Stockton and Darlington Railway, opened in 1825, was primarily constructed to
carry coal from the south western part of the coal field to Stockton for coastal
export. George Stephenson, and later his son Robert, were thus among the early
founders of the railway system which needed engineering for the construction of
its locomotives and also ironfounding for the production of rail-track.

Coal was shipped, particularly from the Tyne, in enormous quantities and shipbuilding was carried out along that river, and around Sunderland. A quarter of a
century after the opening of the Stockton and Darlington Railway, another
significant event took place, namely the launching at Jarrow in 1852 of the
John Bowes, the first iron-built screw steam collier. The *John Bowes* also had the
advantage of another new development, for she was designed to operate by water
ballast. Instead of carrying heavy waste or low-grade materials when travelling in
ballast, she could take on water which was later pumped out by her steam engines.
The end of the need for unsightly ballast heaps along the Tyne banks had come.
But other industries were equally threatened, for the glass industry had come north

in the seventeenth-century seeking cheap coal in place of charcoal, and also because of the cheap transport of bulk materials which would be brought in as ballast. The pottery industry had also benefited in this way from the great fleet of colliers, always needing to return to Newcastle in ballast.

The growth of the ports along the coast of Northumberland and Durham is another feature of the region's history which has greatly affected its people. Newcastle, the furthest point downstream at which the Tyne could be bridged, can trace its history to the Romans and until after the first World War its industries and its population continued to grow. Downstream the banks of the Tyne must have ranked among the most populated and industrially developed in the country, with shipyards, engineering works, chemical works, glass-houses and potteries. For long Newcastle was the unchallenged centre of the North, until Middlesbrough (a group of four farmhouses until 1830) was planned and rapidly developed Seaton Sluice in Northumberland is an early example of an artificial harbour, built between 1761 and 1764 by Thomas Delaval, local industrialist and coal-owner, and Seaham Harbour was built between 1828 and 1831 by Lord Londonderry for coal export. This eminent though far from popular coal-owner decided that his port should have beside it an attractive town and commissioned the architect John Dobson accordingly. Dobson, as we shall see in a later chapter, played an important part in the nineteenth-century splendour of Newcastle's central streets.

But not all northern town planning was of the last century, for several new towns of recent years are now flourishing, including Peterlee, Aycliffe and Washington in Durham, and Cramlington in Northumberland. Other towns elsewhere in the region, such as Alnwick or Barnard Castle, have remained relatively static generally as small market towns. They have survived without too many drastic changes in this century and help to give us a glimpse of what the rural North-East was like more than a century ago. Yarm, on the Tees, also shows what an inland port of the eighteenth century was like, when sailing ships took several days to beat their way upriver to its quays.

At that time most of the North-East was rural, as indeed most of western Durham and the larger part of Northumberland still are. We must not let our consideration of industrial and transport developments blind us to the essentially rural character of the larger part of the region, and until about 1830, one third of the 'labouring classes' of County Durham were engaged in agriculture alone. In Northumberland, farming was a prosperous occupation, as the large and well-built farmsteads testify. And these farms needed many farm workers, as their adjoining terraces of hind-houses also demonstrate. Northumberland was particularly well placed to benefit from the progressive agricultural activities of southern Scotland in the early and middle years of last century. Features such as the threshing machine (invented in Scotland in 1788), the horse-mill to power it, and the subsequent adoption of steam-threshing all show the influence of lowland Scottish progress.

Meanwhile in County Durham cattle breeding had gone on apace and the Durham Shorthorn, though now much less popular as a breed, was at one time believed to be an outstanding example of breeding to specific ends—good meat with a heavy milk yield.

So, in the round, we can now see Northumberland and Durham as an isolated area, largely cut off from the rest of England by sheer distance and partly by hills within which lay part of its eventual wealth. In prehistoric times and through subsequent early centuries it received invaders who were gradually absorbed, bringing with them strange languages which merged and changed to linger as a curious dialect. And as it moved into the nineteenth century it received a great input of labour, first to work its mines and then to operate its machines and factories. These men came, often with their families, from the surrounding countryside, from other mining regions and from Ireland and though they all came with their own dialects, habits and customs, they somehow also merged (perhaps rather as the United States has merged into a nation from many nationalities) to produce an identifiable character. Such a man is sometimes called a 'Geordie', though this tends to mean more specifically a dweller along the Tyne, and the real North-Easterner can be identified from the length of Northumberland to the banks of the Tees. Beyond that lies Yorkshire—a different country. Jack Common (who will again be quoted in Chapter 13) once wrote: 'I was accustomed to hearing only the pure English spoken in Northumberland and on the Tyne and did not know that as you get deeper into Durham a tykey element creeps into the dialect as a sort of warning to the sensitive traveller that the bottomey dumps of Yorkshire are, indeed, evident.'

This, then, is the North-East, and having seen the foundations of the countryside in which the North-Easterner lives and works, let us try and identify some of his characteristics: what *is* different about the North-Easterner?

2 The Shaping of the People

More than five thousand years ago the North-East was probably uninhabited by humans, but around that time a small group of hunter and fisher folk reached the southern Tyne region and began to settle. They were probably related to a larger community of colonists who flourished a little further south in County Durham. They are described by archaeologists as mesolithic people, since they followed the 'Old Stone Age' people in southern England and were later succeeded by the neolithic or 'New Stone Age' people.

In fact it was only when neolithic peoples appeared, around four and a half thousand years ago, that the early activity in Northumberland became more marked. Around this time the local inhabitants began to use polished stone axes and several of these have been found in the North-East, particularly in the two regions which were always favourite areas of early settlement in Northumberland— Coquetdale and Redesdale. Several burial cairns of elongated oval shape have also been discovered in those areas and these are known to be a distinctive feature of the neolithic race. The peoples having this particular cult may well have spread from south-east Scotland rather than from further south in England.

However the beaker folk (so-called on account of their characteristic pottery) invaded the coast around four thousand years ago and gradually spread inland. Like their predecessors they were relatively unadventurous and confined themselves to fairly restricted localities. They certainly reached central Coquetdale and also settled around Rothbury. The distribution of their various remains has been recorded in the North-East and makes it fairly clear that settlement only took place along the river valleys and the coastal plain.

The many cup and ring-marked boulders which have been found in the North East roughly date from this period of, say, 1800 BC. These prehistoric carvings are mostly found in the Fell Sandstone, in the Rothbury and Wooler areas of Northumberland. Boulders and, in some cases, rock outcrops have been carved in concentric circles, which are also associated with hollow cup-like markings and other deep-inscribed lines and grooves. Their function is, of course, unknown, but it is generally thought to have had some religious significance.

Although the beaker folk are sometimes referred to as the Bronze Age people, bronze itself (an alloy of copper and tin) was only introduced late to the North-East, probably after 1000 BC. There is little evidence of the succeeding period, generally referred to as the Iron Age, for although in other parts of the British Isles this was an epoch of intense activity, little seems to have happened in Northumberland and Durham until around the time of the arrival of the Romans. It seems possible that when the Romans first came the local inhabitants were still exponents of a bronze-using culture.

At that time the Votadini were occupying border country in Northumberland and southern Scotland. Here they had numerous hill forts, the greatest of which was Traprain Law near the Forth. These people were probably refugee Celts who had come from further south and were almost certainly the first users of iron to establish themselves north of the Tyne. Meanwhile the Brigantes concentrated their power upon their greatest fortress, at Stanwick, which lies just south of the Tees nor far from the present Scotch Corner. Their area of occupation was generally south of the Tyne. These Celtic people probably did not settle very thoroughly except in their hill forts but they did leave behind them identifiably Celtic words describing the places they knew.

These place names all refer to natural features, and we cannot see any trace of habitation names, yet these words are the first 'living' trace of any north-eastern settlers. They include the names of several rivers such as Alwent, Deerness, Derwent, Don, Team, Tees, Tyne and Wear. Words describing places include Pontop, which is probably parallel to the Welsh word *pant* meaning a valley, to which has been added the Old English word *hop* also meaning a valley. Penshaw is also parallel to the early Welsh word *penn* for a hill. Another word, which subsequently gained a later Old English addition, is that of Cockerton, from the Celtic *kukro* meaning 'crooked', to which was added the Old English word *tun* meaning a homestead or village.

The Roman occupation of the North-East had little effect upon the tribes which occupied this distant country, which has been described as 'the vanishing point of Romanisation', though the Roman roads persisted long after the legions had been withdrawn, and were much used as lines of penetration by both raiding bands and subsequent settlers. However in several places locally, for example along the line of the Wall, a greater degree of Romanisation took place. It was Roman policy that their garrisons should, wherever possible, be supported by the surrounding countryside, thus having an impact on local tribes.

With one exception it seems likely that the Romans did not impose themselves very strongly upon the Celtic population. That one exception seems to have been an exchange of population which was made about the middle of the second century, when the Romans apparently transferred a group of Votadini people into the upper Rhine basin, and brought a number of Rhaetians into the north from the Rhine.

After the Romans finally evacuated Britain, towards the end of the fourth century, the local people seem, for a time, to have maintained some of the Roman traditions and ways of life. However the Angles and Saxons began to invade the north shortly afterwards and gradually imposed themselves upon the region. Around 620 AD the first Anglo Saxon kingdom of Northumbria was established, and by 640 the midland kingdom of Mercia became of primary importance and the others became subject to it. Fifteen years later the King of Northumbria regained leadership of the Anglo Saxons but only for another twenty years or so. During the eighth century that great historian, the Venerable Bede, was working at Jarrow, finishing his most famous work *Ecclesiastical History of the English Nation* in 731 AD and dying there in 735. Towards the end of that century Viking raids on Northumbria began and by the 820s the southern kingdom of Wessex had risen to power and enforced the submission of the king of Northumbria. In the mid-800s the Danes began to invade midland England though they too recognised the supremacy of Wessex. In the early 900s the Vikings moved from the west back into northern England, though by 1000 AD all of England was briefly part of the Danish empire under King Canute.

We may summarise these ins and outs of the Angles, Saxons and other invaders by seeing Northumbria grow out of a confederation of small tribes into two strong groups, the southern one called the Deirans and the northern group the Bernicians. The Tees was probably the southern boundary of the Bernicians and certainly the Tees valley was, after the Scandinavian settlement, debateable land between the Vikings of Yorkshire and the old Anglian settlers to the north. Despite strong kingdoms in the seventh and eighth centuries, which ruled over the whole area, these two divisions were still alive when the Vikings conquered southern Northumbria in the mid-ninth-century.

These various peoples left their marks on our countryside in the way of place names. Thus names ending in *-ingham* (for example Chillingham, Whittingham, Bellingham and Barningham) tend to indicate early settlements of what could be termed the entrance phase. The early Anglian settlement in Northumberland lay along the valleys of the Tyne and the North Tyne, with a scatter in County Durham. The many place name elements, sometimes of later origin which can be identified as Anglian include *ham* (village), *worth* (enclosure or homestead), *wic* (farm or dwelling), *tun* (homestead) and *burh* (a fortified place). We can identify such elements in words like Seaham which means a 'village by the sea', Killing-worth which means 'the enclosure of Cylla's people', Hunwick meaning 'Huna's farm', Washington meaning 'the homestead of Wassa's people' and Bradbury meaning 'the fort built of boards'.

One may digress here, for a moment, to observe that an occupation of a group or race of people can have a marked effect upon its vocabulary. It is said for example that the Bedouin tribe, depending for its very existence upon the camel, has nearly a hundred words for this essential beast, since it is clearly important that the tribesmen should be able to identify and describe its many varieties, colours, conditions and so on. Similarly a Dales shepherd has many more words for his sheep—ewe, gimmer, tup etc.—than a town-dweller would need.

In a similar way we can draw a conclusion from the many words for a settlement, as left behind by the Angles and Saxons who invaded the north more than a thousand years ago. If we observe the number of words meaning homestead or village: *ham, worth, wic, tun, ingham* etc., it becomes clear that these invaders were settlers who took over and gradually improved the agricultural state of the countryside. We can even trace the gradual encroachment which they made into the surrounding woodland, by the frequency of place-names including *lea*, for this indicates clearances which they made in the woods, for further agriculture. Other extensions of the worked land were made into hill country and here herds-men's shelters were constructed, used originally for seasonal pastures and later for more permanent settlements. The word *shiel* means a temporary shelter and hence one can see that Allenshields, near Hunstanworth, was a shelter above the river Alwin. Axwell Park near Winlaton is less obvious, but an early document shows this place-name as Aksheles, incorporating the word *Ac* meaning an oak tree. Axwell therefore indicates the site where originally a shiel or shelter was built up in the hills, at a place where oak trees grew. Another curious name—Unthank—comes from an Old English word meaning 'without leave', in other words a squatter's farm. One occurrence of this name is a farm four miles west of Whittingham in Northumberland and another is a farmstead two miles above Forest-in-Teesdale.

Not only can the names of dwellings and living places be identified from Anglian place names, but we can recognise something of the local fauna of the time. For example the word wolf can be identified in Ushaw and Woolley meaning respectively 'the wolf wood' and 'the wolf vale'. Equally bison can be identified in the name Urpeth which means 'the bisons path' and indeed remains of wild ox have been found in various parts of the county. The stag can be recognised in Harton, which means 'stag hill', in the name of Hart village, and in Hartley in Northumberland, meaning 'the hill of the stags'. Even the corn weevil has been identified in the two place names of Hamsterley, one north-west of Bishop Auckland and the other near Ebchester, both in County Durham.

Scandinavian place names mainly occur in the far south of Durham county, between Barnard Castle in the west and Hart in the east and this is the approximate area of the only Durham wapentake of Sadbergh. Within this area one can find a number of place names ending in *by* which indicates the old Norse word for a village or homestead. Typical examples are Raby, Selaby, Killaby, Ulnaby etc. Sadbergh itself comes from the old Norse *set-berg* indicating 'flat-topped hill'.

There is special sign of a Danish settlement, as distinct from a Norwegian one, in the word *thorp* which is old Danish for an outlying farm. It seems therefore that the most intensive settlement of the Scandinavian peoples was west of Stockton, probably associated with colonisation from the North Riding of Yorkshire.

On the other hand it seems that at one stage there was an intrusion into upper Weardale over the hill tops from western England for such names as Ireshope and Irestone, which appear there and include the old Norse word *iri* meaning 'Irishman'. This was a term used for Norwegian settlers who had come over from Ireland. These names therefore probably indicate a late intrusion from the direction of Alston in Cumberland. In the Stanhope and Wolsingham parishes one also finds the word *gill* occurring (meaning a' ravine or narrow valley'), which also suggests Irish-Norwegian settlement. Such names are even more frequent in upper Teesdale where Norwegian influence is certain. Good examples are Snaisgill indicating 'Sniallr's valley' and Howgill incorporating the old Norse word *holr* meaning 'hollow'.

After that well known date of 1066, when the Normans, a vigorous blend of Viking and Franc, invaded England they quickly moved north to occupy the whole country. However the rising of the north three years later, which led to its ruthless 'harrying', resulted in northern England being almost depopulated for a time. The Scots also apparently took the opportunity of coming south into Northumberland, at a time when the local people were quite unable to fend for themselves. Not surprisingly the Doomsday Survey of 1086 stopped short at the river Tees, though this was not only because the lands to the north were so barren and ravaged that they were not worth recording, but also because the Bishop of Durham was regarded as a semi-independent ruler. Perhaps this is the point at which the north for the first time asserted itself successfully against the rest of England!

We can recognise quite a number of post-Conquest names of French origin in our region including Pallion from the old French *pavillion* meaning 'a tent'. Friars Goose is a particularly interesting name for, despite what it apparently seems to indicate, it in fact refers to *le freregos*. This was the old French word for 'sea holly' a plant now rare in the north, but obviously found along the southern bank of the Tyne to the east of Gateshead in the tenth and eleventh centuries.

The connective *le* of names like Chester-le-Street and Houghton-le-Skerne is simply the French definitive article, remaining after the preceding preposition *in* or *on* had been dropped.

There are other feudal additions to be seen in local place names, for example Coatham Mundeville, Dalton Piercy (once held by the Percy family), Hutton Henry which probably comes from Henry de Essh of around 1380 and Witton Gilbert from Gilbert de Leia of about 1180. It is also interesting to note that the pronounciation of 'Gilbert' still takes the Anglo Norman sound of '*J*'. This name is still locally pronounced 'Jilbert' despite its modern spelling.

The name Durham is of particular interest. Around 1000 AD it was known as Dunholm from the old English word *dun* meaning a hill and the Scandinavian word *holm* meaning an island; in other words an island with a hill. Durham is of course built on a rocky hill nearly surrounded by the Wear and this is accordingly a vivid and accurate description of the siting of the city. The liquid sound was later hardened by the Norman invaders to the sound 'r' and they wrote it as Dureaume in 1170 AD. By 1300 it was being written as *Duram*. Thus here we have an example of an Anglo-Danish name having a French pronounciation and being spelt in an anglicised form!

This rapid tracing of the historical development of settlement in the North-East has brought us to the point of written history, though by no means to the end of place-name innovations. To take a few examples, much waste land was colonised in early mediaeval times and along the valley sides of Weardale is a scatter of settlements. These date between the late twelfth and early fourteenth centuries, with such names as Newlands, Woodcroft and Newlandside. The plan of the Bishop of Durham's deer park is moreover preserved in the village names of Eastgate and Westgate, while to the north is the deserted farmstead of Northgate.

In later years popular fancy seems to have chosen such names as Quebec (a mining village five miles west of Durham) and Botany, a now-ruined farmstead on Romaldkirk Moor in Teesdale. And the word 'colliery' is often found attached to older village names, to distinguish the more recent industrial settlement, such as Boldon Colliery and Trimdon Colliery. Another industrially inspired name is 'winning' meaning the successful completion of a new mine, as for example Esh

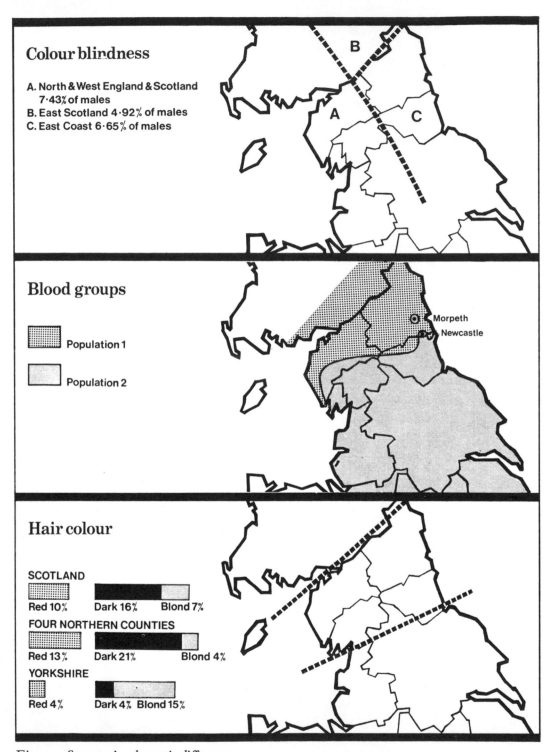

Colour blindness

A. North & West England & Scotland
   7·43% of males
B. East Scotland 4·92% of males
C. East Coast 6·65% of males

Blood groups

Population 1

Population 2

Morpeth
Newcastle

Hair colour

SCOTLAND

Red 10%   Dark 16%   Blond 7%

FOUR NORTHERN COUNTIES

Red 13%   Dark 21%   Blond 4%

YORKSHIRE

Red 4%   Dark 4%   Blond 15%

Fig. 2. Some regional genetic differences.
These maps are based on a paper by Dr Sunderland in the British Association volume on Durham (1970). They are, of course, only approximate. In the third map the percentages of brown hair are not shown.

Winning. Perhaps the most recent place-name is that of Peterlee, the new town named after the famous socialist Peter Lee.

So much for the vivid though often intangible remains of the region's many invasions and historical changes, preserved as countryside place-names. It is now possible, through recent research, to identify something of the very people themselves by traces which they have left within our population. It is widely known that blood can be classified into several groups and these groupings have to be identified before a transfusion can be given. It is perhaps not so well known that certain blood groups are more commonly found in one part of the country than another, and by making a careful examination of the blood groups of people in the North-East, it has been found that there are two 'populations' each with its own predominant blood group. The division between these populations runs roughly along the line of the Tyne, with a curious patch of the more southerly population clinging around Morpeth. These two north-country populations also have links with populations further afield; the more northerly one is not only similar in part to that of Scotland but also has much in common with populations in Iceland. The population of Durham and the south of our region, on the other hand, has much more in common with the blood group types of southern England which themselves link with those of western Europe.

Another regional difference which can be shown statistically is that of hair colouration. The population of Northumberland and Durham, in common also with that of Cumberland and Westmorland has a much higher percentage of dark brown-haired and red-haired people than has the population either to the north in Scotland or to the south of our area.

The task of trying to link these statistical facts with the series of invasions and occupations which the region has undergone over the centuries is, of course, far too complex for consideration here, but it can now be seen that there are still traces of our many forbears in existence around us and with us, if we only know how and where to look.

3 Hill Farmers

Life in the upper dales and surrounding hills can never have been easy. It has, however, bred a rugged independence and a curious gentleness in the hill farmers which can still be sensed on market day in a dales market town like Barnard Castle, or at a farm sale when everyone gathers in much the same way that they might at a large funeral—fairly serious, but glad of the opportunity to meet friends and neighbours.

Probably the earliest method of farming these hills with their *cleughs* and *riggs* (valleys and ridges) was by transhumance; that is by seasonal migration. In its most remote origins this custom may derive from the pasture management of nomadic herdsmen, but in later years it became a more localised way of using inaccessible pastures or land unusable in winter. In 1599 Camden visited Redesdale in Northumberland and noted that 'here every way round about in the *wasts* as they term them you mey see as it were the ancient *Nomads,* a martiall kinde of men, who from the moneth of Aprill unto August, lye out scattering and summering (as they tearme it) with their cattell in little cottages here and there which they call *sheales* and *shealings*'.

During the Middle Ages summer pasturing was a widespread practice over much of northern England, but it only survived in a few areas into the sixteenth and seventeenth centuries. Differential use of pastures in summer and winter indeed continues, but it now involves the movement of animals, by sale, from farm to farm, not a migration of people and stock.

During their summer occupation of the high pastures the herdsmen needed shelter and not surprisingly we find old place-names indicating temporary huts and sheds, such as 'shield' from the Middle English word *schele* meaning a hut or shelter. (Espershields in Northumberland means 'East Burntshiel: the eastern burnt hut'.) This word has close links with the old Norse word *skali,* now found as 'Scale' in Cumberland and Westmorland and with the same meaning of a temporary building. Another old Norse word with a similar meaning is *erg* and although this also is commonly found in the North-West (Medlar in Lancashire: 'middle shieling';

Torver also in Lancashire: 'peat shieling' and Winder in Cumberland), it is very rare in the North-East. Eryholme, a village on the southern bank of the Tees south of Darlington, is perhaps the sole north-eastern example of this Norse word. And it may well be that the north-eastern flanks of the Pennine hills were not used for transhumance before the twelfth century. This could explain the absence of the Norse *erg* in an area where other old Norse names occur.

While on this topic of upland place-names one may mention a few others to be found on the north-eastern hills such as 'Steel' meaning a steep slope (from the Old English *stigol* a stile or steep place). This word still lingers in the dialect, as also does 'Tod' meaning a fox (Todburn Steel is a farm a few miles south-east of Hexham); 'Law' is an old English word for a hill and 'warden' has a similar though more specific meaning as 'a watch-hill'.

The rural buildings of the Northern Border country of Bewcastle Fells in Cumberland and parts of Tynedale in Northumberland have been surveyed by the Royal Commission on Historical Monuments, which found that the principal use of these moors had been the grazing of stock, many parts having been too wet for sheep, until at least the late eighteenth-century, when improved breeds and better drainage extended the range of hill sheep farming. The only other evidence of human activities are some nineteenth-century coal-mines, a few earlier bell pits, small quarries, turbaries (for peat-getting), illicit whisky stills and, from the early nineteenth century, shooting-butts.

Moving down the dales to the flanks of the larger valleys such as Weardale and Teesdale, sometimes described by geographers as the lead dales due to their past predominant industry, one finds that within living memory the three chief crops have been peat, hay and wool. To some extent the harvesting of these crops could be staggered, though life was very busy from late May to September. Peat, the chief fuel for isolated cottages on the nearly treeless hills, was cut in late May and June and then left to dry until September. Sheep clipping would begin in June and continue into July, while the hay would be cut in July and probably got in during August. In recent years the sheep would be dipped in October to rid them of skin-infesting parasites. Through the last century the more laborious hand-process of 'salving' or 'greasing' was carried out, whereby each sheep was held on a salving stock or wooden trestle, the hair parted and a sticky mixture of grease and Stockholm tar rubbed in. During November and December the ewes would be run with the ram, and lambing would take place in April after the worst of the snows had passed.

In 1963 I talked to a very old man, Jasper Stephenson of Newbiggin Farm near Blanchland. He remembered what he called 'greasing time', when the sheep were treated with a mixture of Stockholm tar and butter. They used to do it, he said, in the byres in October and the light wasn't too good, so they had a rope stretched along the byre with loops in it and a tallow dip in each loop. ('If they didn't snuff

Fig. 3. Sheep marking and salving.
In the salving bowl (made of wood and held by the rough handle) a mixture of Stockholm tar and butter was kept, for greasing the sheep. Pitch was heated up and used to mark the sheep after shearing, and the mark is that of Tom Dent of Mickleton. Horns were branded by hot irons. The owner of this brand is unknown, but it was found at Brignall, near Barnard Castle.

the wick before it burnt down to the rope, the rope took fire, and the whole kaboosh came down for the length of the byre'.)

The sheep were greased to waterproof the fleece which would be very heavy when wet, and also to kill the *kades* (grubs of the sheep fly). Butter was mixed in with the tar to make it better to spread. Each man had a sheep-stool in the byre, in a long line, and he turned the sheep up on the sheep-stool and tied its legs. Then he *shed* the wool from the tail right up to the neck—that is, he parted the thick wool with his thumbs and took a quantity of grease and rubbed it into the skin. Then he started again, one or one and a half inches away and put another line up the wool. This was very difficult on the neck, where the wool was like a mat, but the neck was just the place where the kades laid their eggs, so it was very important to shed 'up to the lugs' (as far as the ears).

Mr Stephenson then went on to recite a dialect poem about this farming activity. It was, he said, a poem which he had learned from his father and which he believed to have been written about 1860. There had been two brothers, Michael and Jack Anderson who were shepherds on the farm called Nookton next to his. One brother, Michael, had stayed on the farm and the other had gone into the Baptist Ministry. He wrote this poem from London, whilst obviously yearning to be back on the farm:

> *'My mind it's a fleein*
> *away to the North—just to see what ye're deein.*
> *Whiles howkin on here and rivin si fast*
> *A' think mesel there, as A' was in days past.'*

He goes on to recall:

> *'Aboot all kinds o' sheep that gans on the fell.*
> *Ye begin with the hoggs—Ah how they lie scowlin!*
> *An' the kades fro' their backs, how they come crowlin!*
> *They shed varry teeuf and gow the thumbs wark . . .'*

After greasing went out of fashion, Mr Stephenson recalled, dipping took over as a means of killing the kades. But the water soaked the fleeces and so they used to put on brown grease from Bradford. This was grease taken out of the sheared fleeces by the Bradford wool-scourers, who then sold it back to the sheep farmer. 'And now', said Mr Stephenson, 'I don't think there are many people putting grease in, but they are putting whale oil in'.

The peat harvest was once essential to the hill farmers who lacked any other fuel, but this is now no longer so. And although one is always hesitant to state categorically that some old custom or tradition has completely died out, it does seem that peat-getting is no longer practised in the north of England, except for some isolated individual cutting a little as much for his own amusement as for use as a cheap fuel.

A few recollections have been recorded from fairly elderly people which will serve to indicate the kind of skills and equipment in use in the early years of this century. From upper Teesdale Mr Harry Beadle of Forest in Teesdale recently said that although he could not recall full-scale peat cutting he could still remember when almost every family in upper Teesdale obtained a quantity of peat with which to supplement the coal that they obtained from the rail-head at Middleton in Teesdale station. Incidentally if they did not collect their coal from the rail-head they might have got it by horse and cart from small coal pits in the Woodland area nearby. Mr Beadle described a variety of spades which he remembered being used including one illustrated (fig. 4) from Harwood. This is regarded as a typical spade, though there was a wide variety of shape and size, since they were made by local blacksmiths, each with his own particular fancy. A spade of this kind was used to cut the hard black variety of peat, but was unsuitable for the rougher more fibrous type. The pieces which were cut would measure about four inches square and were of various lengths depending on the texture.

Mr Beadle recollects that the rough fibrous peat was normally cut by an ordinary peat spade which had to be very sharp and sometimes a hay spade would be used. The *peats* would be about twelve or fifteen inches long by eight or nine inches wide and three or four inches thick. At *peat-cutting* time, which was usually about June when the moors had dried out a little, the man of the house would engage in the cutting and women and children would carry the peats across onto the *bent* or heather where they were laid flat until such time as they had dried sufficiently to be *set up*. Each family had its own recognised place on the moor and no-one would think of encroaching on another person's *peat pot* and drying ground. After about two months of drying, during which time the hay crop would be gathered, the peat would be carried by sacks to the nearest point to which a horse and cart or sledge could be brought. From there they were taken home and stacked indoors if possible. However in view of the small amount of accommodation at most of the farms they were usually stacked against a field wall adjacent to the house, so that air could circulate and dry the peat still further. Some of the peat dried so hard that it could only be broken by hammer, while the rough fibrous kind often remained fairly soft.

Other Teesdale informants have described how peat was cut or 'gathered' immediately after the cattle were turned out in May and before the beginning of the hay harvest at the end of July. Every farm had its right of turbary (that is, the right to dig 'turf' or peat) included in the enclosure agreement for the Parish.

'Peatin' was a seasonal event in which all the family took part. The men dug

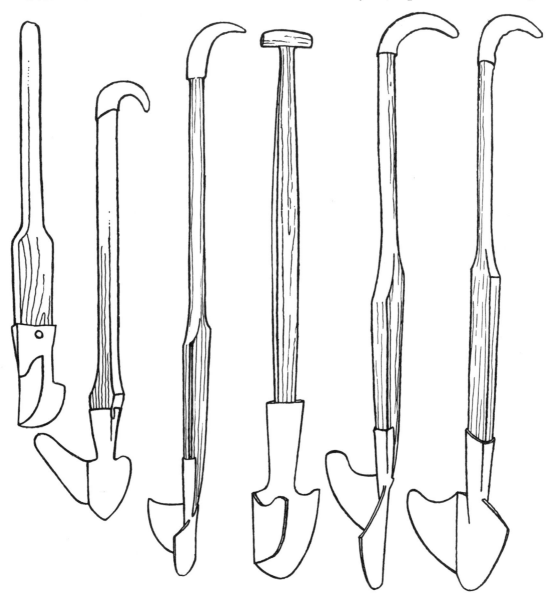

Fig. 4.   Northern peat spades.
These come from Teesdale and Weardale. That on the left has lost its horn handle, and on the right are two views of the same spade. Peat spades generally have the 'wing' on the right, but not invariably so.

from the *peat haggs* and trundled it by barrow to the drying grounds where the women *footed* or stacked the peat. The top turf was cut off with a *flaughting spade* or paring spade and this was usually kept for kindling the fire. It was important that the peat cutting area was properly drained and a channel was cut for this at the foot of the bank. The top turfs might be laid over the area where the men stood and after a time these became compressed and provided a firm solid platform on which to work.

In earlier times the peats were out out with winged peat spades, of the kind shown on fig. 4. Mr Douglas Hind confirms that there seem to have been two different types of spade. Firstly those fitted with a broad crosspiece handle (and frequently with the broadest of winged blades). These were used for making the primary vertical cut and were handled by a man standing on top of the bank.

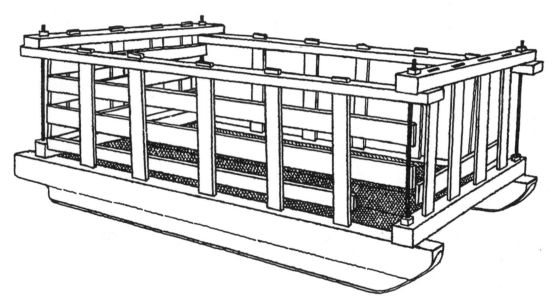

Fig. 5. Peat sledge.
Because of the rough terrain peat, after being cut and dried, was brought down from the moor in sledges like this one.

Secondly there was another type of winged peat spade which was used more horizontally, at right angles to the face of the bank, in order to cut out the peat brick which had already been loosened by the first vertical cut.

The peat blocks as they were cut were flicked from the web of the spade on to the sideless peat barrow and then taken to the drying grounds. Here the women and children would 'foot' the peat or build them into small beehive-shaped stacks.

The blocks were then left on the moor until after haymaking when they were led to the farmstead by horse and cart. About forty cart-loads of peat would be taken and the family would use about a cart-load a week. At the farmyard the peat might have been stacked in a special peat house, or failing this, in a cart shed. Mrs Thwaites of Baldersdale remembers seeing the cart almost enclosed by the peats stacked up around it for winter use. Mr William Iceton of Romaldkirk recalls peat stacks constructed in the open and thatched with rushes which had been secured by hay-ropes and weights.

Mr Douglas Hind of Hunderthwaite was probably the last person to cut peat in the Teesdale area (in the 1940s) and at that time he never used a winged peat spade. These seem to have gone out of use some time before that. Mr Hind used an ordinary garden spade, cutting his peat into blocks of about a cubic foot and then splitting them down with a hay knife for drying. Mr Iceton remarked that he could remember driving sheep over the fell on a dark night and seeing the glow of the open *peat pots*. This, he thought, was due to phosphorus content in the peat.

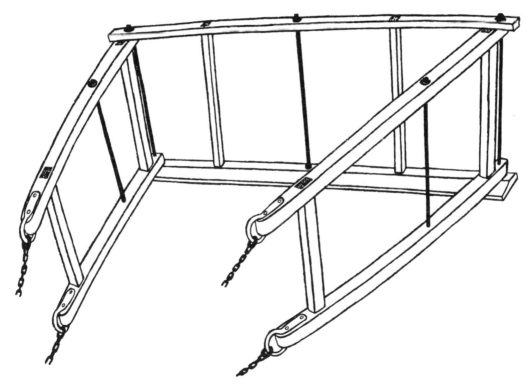

Fig. 6.   A dales wing sweep.
This was used to gather hay, and was pulled behind a horse. See plate 18.

The other chief crop on the hills was hay, and this, unlike peat, is still gathered in and still with much manual labour. 'Hay-timing' probably lingers in many childhood memories on account of the fine weather—so rare on the hills—which is needed to get in the hay successfully.

The 'long scythe' favoured in Weardale and Teesdale for grass cutting is one of the forbears of the now-ubiquitous' 'American' scythe. For whereas the latter has a steam-curved handle to fit partway round the body, the old Dales scythe handle could be seven or eight feet long and completely straight. In keeping with this the blade was around five feet long and its length measured to match the worker

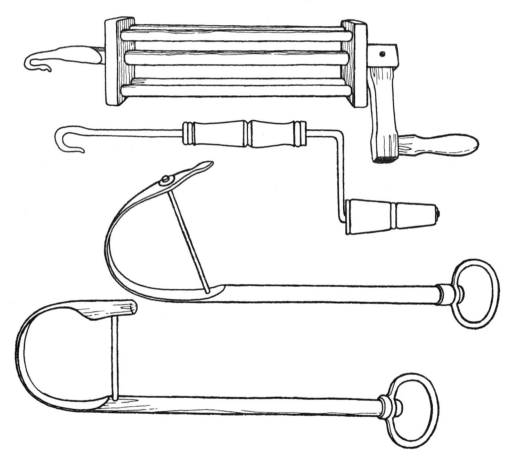

Fig. 7. Straw or hay rope-twisters.
The upper two examples are fairly easy to understand, but the lower two, from central Northumberland had to be attached to the man's belt by the small loop and a twist was applied to the straw rope by dextrous rotation of the curved wooden pieces. In dialect these latter implements are called thra'
crooks.

by placing the heel of the scythe on the ground (the place where the blade meets the shaft), with the blade point upwards. The tip of the blade should then reach to the man's chin.

After the hay was cut it was raked into windrows to dry and probably turned once or twice depending on how dry the weather was. If the weather looked doubtful and there might not be time to get it safely in, it would be raked into cocks and these would later be gathered into pikes. On the other hand, if the weather seemed likely to hold fair the hay might be raked straight into pikes. The gate sweep would then come into play, to bring together the hay into still larger piles. A gate-sweep is, as its name suggests, little more than a single gate-like wooden structure with a strengthened bottom bar shaped to help the scraping action as the sweep was dragged along upright by a horse, with the driver behind. What looks like a development of the gate sweep, and was certainly easier to use, was the wing-sweep (fig. 6) and several dales farms still have one of these, though they are now infrequently used.

The hay pikes were brought down to the hay barn by a pike bogey, another horse-drawn implement, but this time on wheels. The body was low-slung and quite flat. It could be tilted down to the ground at the back and a rope was thrown round the pike which was then winched, by a double-handed roller, up on to the bogey. The body was then levelled up on the wheels and drawn down to the building.

On the very steepest fields where even a pike bogey might be difficult to handle, a large sledge was used. These are now quite scarce, but occasionally in very heavy snow one might be brought out and used at the very top of the dale to help get fodder out to the sheep.

4 Lead Miners of the Dales

The highest part of the northern Pennines is a barren expanse of moorlands, bounded to the north by the Tyne Gap, to the west by the Eden Valley and to the south by the Stainmore Pass. To the east lies the Durham coalfield. This wild but beautiful plateau lies mostly between one and two thousand feet above sea level and the mining communities which were once scattered across its dales have left behind them traces of some of the most isolated settlements in the country. An outstandingly important reason for the colonisation of this inhospitable land was the presence of rich deposits of lead ore. The upper valleys of the rivers Tees, Wear, Derwent, Allen and South Tyne are often referred to by geographers as the 'lead dales', though farming and quarrying have also helped to provide occupations for the inhabitants and these are today the principle sources of employment for the much reduced population.

Traditionally the lead-miner's cottage was a tiny farmstead with barn, hayloft and living quarters all under one roof. Although now the cultivation of grass and the rearing of sheep and cattle are the sole farming activities in the dales, during the lead-mining era arable farming was practised at heights above 700 feet. These smallholdings not only provided an additional source of income for the miner, but in the later nineteenth century they also provided employment for women, who, by then, were not being employed in the mining industry.

During the eighteenth and nineteenth centuries not only was Britain the world's largest producer of lead, but the lead dales were the principle lead-mining area of Britain and the dales were scattered not only with mines and their associated buildings, but with ore dressing plants and smelting works. Unlike other extractive industries such as ironstone mining and limestone quarrying, the lead industry was not simply an extractive one. It created other employment, often for women and children, by the use of machinery and buildings in which the ore was prepared through to the finished metal. The history of this lead-mining region also provides a refreshing contrast to the history of the nearby Durham and Northumberland coalfield. Not only have there never been great disasters to compare with such accidents as those at Felling Colliery in 1812 when 92 lives were lost, or Hartley Colliery in 1862 when 204 lives were lost or Seaham in 1880 when 164 lives were lost. Equally there was an absence of class conflict of the kind typified by the coal miners' strikes of 1832 and 1844. Indeed the history of trade unionism among the coal miners is not found repeated with the lead miners. The lead mining companies provided housing, schools, libraries and medical services for the support of their labour force. Yet the independence and freedom prized by the miners was mostly left untouched. (How much these differences are due to the different treatment of the men and how much to the different mining techniques it is impossible to say. But whereas coal miners worked crouching in endless low seams of monotonous constancy, lead miners gambled with veins of unknown value. Perhaps these differences affected their views on life?)

The great development of the lead industry in England began early in the eighteenth century and by the middle of that century Britain was the world's leading producer. The lead industry benefited moreover from the enoromous expansion of British trade during the eighteenth century and at the same time lead began to be more and more used as the pace of technological development increased. It was needed for piping, for building materials, for printing type and, a little later, as a base in the paint industry. Consequently several ancilliary industries also developed along the banks of the Tyne during the late eighteenth and early nineteenth centuries. There were the Tyne Lead Works at Hebburn, St Anthony's lead Works at Newcastle, the Patent Shot Works at Elswick and other works at Willington, Howden and Ouseburn. However towards the end of the nineteenth century discoveries of rich lead deposits in the United States and development of lead-mining in Spain resulted in much cheaper production than could be attained in Britain, resulting inevitably in the collapse of the British lead-mining industry. The price of lead fell, for example, from an average of twenty-one pounds per ton in the 1850s to about nine pounds per ton in the 1890s, a figure at which most British mines could not economically produce. Mines in the Nenthead area were the most fortunate, for they also had rich zinc deposits and the price of zinc increased at the time when the price of lead was dropping, hence cushioning the worst effects of the collapse of the lead industry there. However, in the rest of the Pennines and in the rest of the country, lead-mining had practically ceased by the end of the nineteenth century. The lead dales have subsequently suffered heavy depopulation and the reduced villages, decayed farmsteads, deserted mine workings and smelt works, abandoned dressing floors and lost pack-horse tracks and railways systems are the most notable features of the landscape-remains of a once great industry and monuments to the people who worked in it.

Lead has been formed in the earth under entirely different conditions from those which have created coal and in consequence mining methods are different too. Coal is found in relatively horizontal seams, of varying thickness up to six or seven feet, and extending at a constant thickness often over many square miles, whereas lead ore is found in nearly vertical veins which can vary considerably in width from a few inches to many feet. The main problem in a coal mine is that of supporting the roof while the coal is removed, whereas in a lead mine the problem is to provide a floor from which the miner can work while extracting the ore. A shaft would be sunk and from this various levels driven into the ore body. From these levels the miner could work upwards or downards, constructing timber staging wedged between the vein walls in order to provide platforms. The ore, or *bouse* as it has been locally known, was thrown down to a tramway level, where tubs could be filled and driven either directly out through an adit onto the hillside, or to the foot of a shaft. The waste material was stacked on the wooden floors, and known as *deads*. It is these platforms stacked with many hundreds of tons of deads which create the greatest hazard to exploring a mine today. It did mean, however, that lead mines were saved the enormous waste heaps to be found outside coal

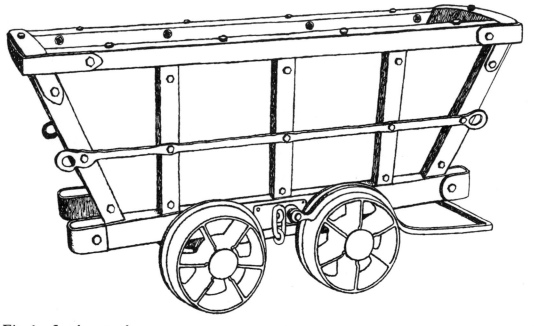

Fig. 8.   *Lead ore truck.*
This, drawn underground by a horse, was used to bring out the bouse *or lead ore, from the Nenthead area. Contrast this with the coal truck (Fig. 23).*

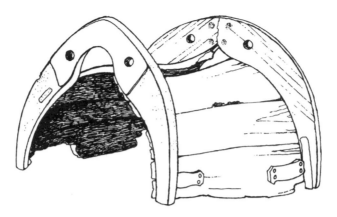

Fig. 9.   Pack saddle for carrying lead.
This was found in the saddle-house at Egglestone and would be used on a 'gallowa' bringing lead down to Darlington from the Egglestone smelt mills last century.

mines. The only waste heaps associated with lead mines are those from the washing floor, left after the ore has been separated from other associated minerals and prepared for smelting.

The men working in the lead veins were paid a price according to the amount of ore which they sent out of the mine. This was measured by the *bing*, a bing being eight hundredweights. The miners usually worked in *partnerships* of from two to twelve men and a partnership would enter into a bargain with the mine agent to raise ore at a certain price in some particular part of the mine. Other men such as joiners, blacksmiths, woodmen, stonemasons and enginewrights were paid at a daily or weekly rate for their work.

Like all mining, the work was dangerous, though there were never the major accidents of the kind occurring in coal mines. However diseases associated with the actual mineral were common and some indication of these can be obtained from a report given by a Dr Peacock in 1864 to the Royal Commission on Mines. He referred to a conversation he had had with some men in the Burtree Pasture Mine:

'they said that the bad air made them feel dizzy, sometimes adding, 'as if they had been in liquor', caused violent headache, and made them feel sleepy, so that they could scarcely keep awake, and took all the power out of their limbs. Sometimes, they said they became quite faint, and I was told that they occasionally had "fits" when working in bad air, and had to be carried out. Not infrequently they felt sick and would vomit violently on coming to the surface; and they suffered from pains in the bowels, constipation or diarrhoea; were much prostrated, and had little or no appetite for their food on getting home'.

Today we would realise that these men were suffering from acute lead poisoning.

Many of the mines were a considerable distance from the nearest settlement and men had to walk a long distance to get to work. Others would seek lodgings near the mine in a neighbouring farmstead, or stay at the company's lodging *shop*. These shops were severely overcrowded and insanitary and considered with some justification to be more harmful than the mines themselves. In 1842 William Eddy gave evidence to the Commission on the Employment of Children:

'Our lodging-rooms were such as not to be fit for a swine to live in. In one house there were 16 bedsteads in the room upstairs, and 50 occupied these beds at the same time. We could not always get all in together, but we got in when we could. Often 3 at a time in a bed and 1 at the foot. . . . After I had been there two years, rules were laid down and two men were appointed by the master to clean the house upstairs twice a week. . . . The breathing at night when all were in bed was dreadful. The men received more harm from the sleeping-places than from the work.'

After the ore had been mined it was brought out and tipped in *bouse teams*. These comprised a series of partitioned bays, where the ore mined by the different partnerships was stored separately, in order that their earnings could be calculated. Next the bouse was broken into small pieces so that the heavier galena or lead ore could be separated from the waste stone and minerals which had surrounded it. This breaking was at one time carried out by women, particularly on certain types of ore which were quite soft and could be broken by striking the lump of ore with a kind of flat-faced hammer, known as a *bucker*. The crushed bouse was then sieved in a tub of water, the heavier galena falling to the bottom, and the lighter waste material being washed away on top. The ore was then crushed still further and washed in a more vigorous flow of water. This washing was done by boys—the washerboys, who had a tedious and miserably cold wet task.

During the late eighteenth and early nineteenth centuries the dressing of lead ore was improved and most of the processes were mechanised. Thus the large crushing mill to be found still standing in Upper Weardale, at Killhope, is one built around 1860. The large water wheel drove a series of grinding wheels and the bouse was dropped between these from a hopper, rather along the lines of an enormous coffee grinder. The ore was then washed mechanically by a variety of complex machines known as buddles.

Although in the eighteenth century women had worked on the dressing floors

1. One of two new breeds, 'Puffing Billy' was built in 1813 by William Hedley of Wylam, Northumberland, for hauling coal from a local colliery. Several early experimental locomotives were designed in the North-East in the early years of the nineteenth century.

2. The other was the Durham Shorthorn, a northern breed produced at a time when farmers were seeking improved efficiency, and the Durham Ox was probably the most famous individual of this breed.

3. Not unattractive ruins of a nineteenth-century colliery on the moors at Stublick, near Langley in Northumberland. The chimney in the distance is the terminal of a long lead smelt-mill flue from Langley.

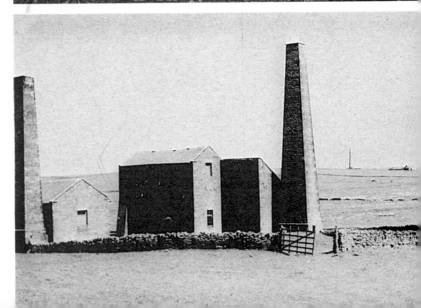

4. *Eighteenth-century lime kilns by the side of the tiny harbour at Beadnell on the Northumberland coast. These are now preserved by the National Trust.*

5. *At Ridsdale near the A68 in Northumberland, this great building looks a little like the keep of a border castle, but was originally a blowing engine house of ironworks built in the 1830s.*

6. *Causey Arch, built in 1727 carried a horse-drawn colliery wagonway across the Tanfield Burn in County Durham. It crosses a hidden and well-wooded narrow valley.*

7. *Near Corbridge, this 'bottle-kiln', named by its shape, was used to make pottery last century.*

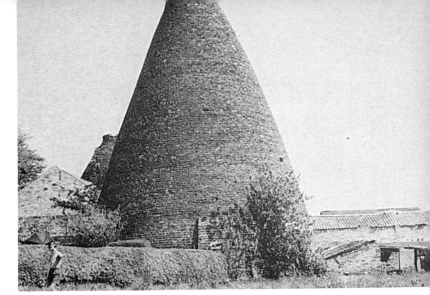

8. *In upper Weardale at Killhope where lead-ore was extracted last century, this large water-wheel was constructed to drive an ore-crushing plant.*

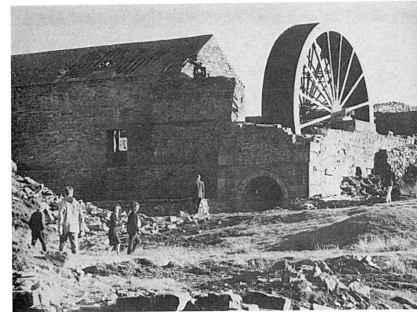

UPLAND AGRICULTURE

9. *Digging peat in upper Weardale early this century.*

10. *Preparing to cut the hay near St John's Chapel, Weardale, about 1912.*

11. *Sheep clipping at Whitefield Bothel, Northumberland in 1894.*

12. *A butter worker in use near Blanchland. After butter had been made in the barrel churn on the left, it was 'worked' over by a wooden ribbed roller to get rid of the butter milk and to work in the salt.*

13. *Pig-killing was quite an event!*

14. *Heather was used for thatching in the hills where it was known as* black thack, *but little now remains. Here are two small barns. This one is near Baldersdale, in upper Teesdale.*

15. *Heather-thatched barn at Broomley, near Stocksfield.*

16. *A load of hay being roped down on a pike bogy.*

17. *Getting in the hay by sledge at St John's Chapel, Weardale.*

18. *Hay being gathered with the use of a wing sweep in Weardale, about 1915.*

LEAD MINING IN THE DALES

19. *Interior of a smelt mill at Rookhope. Left to right, Bob Oliver, old Jack Lowery and Herb Lowery. Molten lead is being poured into a two-wheeled mould.*

20. *Washing tables at a lead-ore preparation plant probably at Nenthead. After separating out the coarser pieces, very fine particles were trickled and washed over these circular 'tables'.*

21. *Tubs of lead-ore being pulled out from a mine on Rotherhope Fell, 1910.*

22. *A date-stone of 1668 above the doorway of 'New House', in Baldersdale, a tributary to Teesdale.*

23. *Another dated doorhead, of 1705, from Baldersdale. This came from the cottage at Hunderthwaite.*

COTTAGES

24. *This very superior doorhead, of 1752, is at High Green, Mickleton in upper Teesdale.*

25. *This oak collar-beam from a roof-truss shows something of the massive construction of an 'upper-cruck'. It came from the now-demolished Old Manor House at Escomb.*

26. *The cottage at Crooks Altar, Weardale, shown in Fig. 12; seen from the west.*

27. *The Crooks Altar Cottage, Weardale, with cow-house below; shown in Fig. 12, seen from the south.*

28. *Fell Close Cottage: although now mostly roofed in corrugated iron, this cottage retains several original features including a heather thatched porch and a studded door.*

30. *A studded early seventeenth-century oak door at Fell Close Cottage near Consett; shown in Fig. 13.*

29. *A small pele tower at Ninebanks, Allendale, Northumberland.*

31. *Cottages at Edmond-byers half a century ago. That on the right still had its heather thatch, or 'black thack'.*

LOWLAND VILLAGES AND LOWLAND FARMING

32. *Oxen were used for farm work long before horses, and their use persisted longer than might have been expected in some rural areas.*

33. *Two show horses at Wolsingham together with their prizes.*

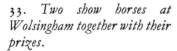

34.   *Steam threshing near Dinsdale in about 1890.*

35.   *Seasonal labour on a farm in the Mitford area of Northumberland around 1870. Women, girls and boys were taken on for potato and turnip harvesting, at haytime and for stone-picking in the spring.*

36. *Steam threshing at Northallerton, Yorkshire, in 1907.*

37. *First prize for a decorated horse in full harness at Shotley Bridge, about 1920.*

38. *Milk being delivered by a horse-drawn 'float', in Northumberland about 1920.*

39. *Logging at Wooler, Northumberland, in 1930.*

40. *A logging camp at Shotley Bridge during the First World War.*

RURAL CRAFTS

41. *Tyring a wooden wheel. After a wooden wheel had been made (itself a highly skilled and exacting process), an iron tyre was welded and fitted on, being first expanded by the heat of a fire and then quickly cooled when fitted, by throwing on water.*

42. *A smithy doorway now preserved at Brancepeth, County Durham. Several decorative doorways of this type can still be seen in the north, perhaps the best-known one being at Ford in Northumberland, dated 1863. Another, at Roxby not far from Whitby in North Yorkshire is dated 1858.*

43. *A blacksmith at work near Barnard Castle. The smith's box, in the foreground, held all his tools and nails conveniently at hand.*

44. *Rope making has now disappeared as a craft, for the hand process could not compete with the speed of machines. It was a lengthy task since the maker had to walk the length of his rope twelve or fourteen times during the process. This photograph was probably taken during the 1920s, at Chester le Street.*

45. *The skills of the tinplate worker have now almost disappeared, but here are several examples of the trade made by Mr Gleason, seen in his shop at Durham about 1911.*

46. *Coopers are still at work at several breweries, but in reducing numbers and generally only repairing rather than making barrels. This photograph (by courtesy of Scottish & Newcastle Breweries), shows a barrel-stave being planed on a jointer plane: the only kind of woodworking plane which is used when lying stationary, with the sole uppermost (or, one might say, 'upside down').*

47. *Robert Ferguson, shoe maker at St John's Chapel, Weardale. He is holding the shoe by means of a loop of rope into which he presses his left foot.*

Fig. 10. *Woman crushing lead ore.*
This illustration comes from a mid-nineteenth-century book: Ure's Dictionary of Arts, Manu-facturers and Mines, *and shows a bucker being used to crush the ore before it is washed.*

of the northern Pennines, during the nineteenth century this practice generally ceased and the work was reserved for men and boys. The youngest boys, aged between nine and eleven years would be employed picking out stones from the ore before it was first crushed. After their first year they were given heavier work such as wheeling the bouse and the deads. In their fourth year they graduated to

Fig. 11. *Lead ingot mould.*
After smelting, the lead was poured into a mould, ready for transport down the valley for sale. This damaged mould was found in a scrap yard at Birtley, Co. Durham and probably came from the Elswick Lead Works.

using the various mechanical separators and after seven years on the dressing floor they would have become familiar with the minerals extracted from the mine and were then either employed as mastermen washers or taken into the mines as a member of a partnership.

The work on the dressing floor depended upon a continuous supply of running water, for this was required both for the operation of water wheels and for the washing of the ore. Small reservoirs were constructed in the hills around the dressing floor thus making it unlikely that work would be interrupted except by severe drought in summer or freezing of the water in winter. Thus during the winter months the older boys, unable to work on the dressing floors, were often taken into the mines and the younger boys sent to one of the schools in the area. Some of the mining companies, and particularly the Commissioners of Greenwich Hospital, provided schools long before they became available to most other working-class children in the country.

Though far from acceptable by today's standards, the working day of the washer-boy on the lead dressing floor was no doubt an enviable one compared with boys in the coalfield. He would be generally expected to work from about seven in the morning to seven in the evening and on Saturday worked only half a day. The work was not dangerous but could be particularly unpleasant out on the open floor in cold wet conditions.

The following pieces of evidence are taken from the Children's Employment Commission of 1842 and relate to the Allenheads lead mine. Thomas Vickars was aged twelve and had been washing ore for two summers. Sometimes, he said, he worked until midnight and had done this perhaps nine or ten times since he had been at Allenheads, and perhaps four or five times until eight or nine o'clock at night. He had been off for a few days with a cold. He worked in the winter when it was fresh for about seven or eight weeks. His father was dead and had worked in the mines. Thomas said that he could read and was able to write his name. He did not now go to school, but went to church every Sunday. He added that he got thick clothing in winter and fetched his dinner with him.

Another witness was Robert Archer who thought that he was aged seventeen. He had been dressing ore for seven summers and had worked until midnight many times every summer. He never worked till midnight except at the grinding mill, but worked late there because there was a good deal of water in the evening. The water wheel made the work long, and it was always at the back end of summer, not so much in the fore end. When he was working until eight o'clock or so he was not grinding and to make up for it was allowed to go away early on Saturday. The work, he said, hurt some of the young ones but he thought their health was good in general. He had sometimes been off work, from a bad head and such like, but not, he thought, from the work. He could not read at all, could not write at all, had never been at school for more than a quarter and went to no school at the time of his interview, but he sometimes went to church.

To return to the treatment of the ore; after it had been purified by being dressed and washed it was ready for smelting, a process whereby the chemical constituents were separated and the purified lead obtained. This was done by heating the ore on a specially designed hearth and the resultant fumes were carried off to a chimney. This was a relatively skilled process and the smelters represented an aristocracy among the working classes in the dales. They were few in number and tended to retain their skills within a family group. The companies themselves offered special inducements in order to retain the services of these skilled men and at Nenthead, for example, the smelters were provided with better housing than the miners. This housing can still be seen today in Hillersdon Terrace. At Langley the smelters were given land suitable for smallholdings, as an added inducement.

Housing was often built by the mining companies and new villages such as Allenheads and Carrshields were built by the Blackett-Beaumont Company, Nenthead and Garrigill were built by the London Lead Company. The housing to be seen in these villages still gives some indication of the kind of standards provided for the miners. The many chapels in those villages emphasise the importance of the non-conformist religions and the schools, reading rooms and libraries, mainly built during the first half of the nineteenth century, show that this industrial society was considerably more enlightened than many other working class communities.

The Church of England had little influence in the lead dales during the eighteenth century since the parish churches were usually to be found in the old market towns, far from the new mining centres. Thus the nonconformist religions were able to spread their influence more readily. Wesley first preached at Blanchland in March 1747 and Methodism eventually established itself as the principle religion of the dales. From the 1820s the Primitive Methodists, or Ranters as they were known, preached with increasing success and by the late nineteenth century the social classes of the dales had become completely polarised around their religious centres. Management would be found at the church, skilled workers at the Wesleyan chapel and other workers at the Primitive Methodist chapel.

During the eighteenth century small charity schools existed up the dales, but proved inadequate to cope with the rising population. However during the early nineteenth century things greatly improved, in no small part due to the encouragement of three local men: Bishop Barrington, Robert Stagg and Thomas Sopwith.

Bishop Barrington was able to establish four new schools in Weardale alone, at Stanhope, Boltsburn, St John's Chapel and Ireshopeburn. These were all supported additionally by the Beaumont family and were begun in 1819. In that same year Robert Stagg, agent to the London Lead Company, was able to open schools at Nenthead and Middleton. These were available to all children irrespective of whether or not their fathers were employed by the company. By the middle of the nineteenth century Thomas Sopwith, agent of the Beaumont family, had opened schools in Allendale and several, such as those at Allenheads, Carrshield and Sinderhope, still stand as buildings, now mostly used as field study centres by the local education authority. For example, the large building at Carrshield bears on one of its gables the inscription:

CAR SHIELD SCHOOL
Built by and on land belonging to
W. B. BEAUMONT ESQ.
for the education of children
of all religious denominations
1851

Today it carries also a plainer modern notice:

CARRSHIELD EXPEDITION CENTRE

Thomas Sopwith who was responsible, on behalf of the owner Mr Beaumont, for these schools, left a diary covering fifty-six years of his life in 167 volumes. He was land agent in the Alston and adjoining areas from the 1820s to 1871 and keenly interested in engineering progress and social reform. Hence his diary is uniquely important in its concern with everyday mining life. He retained his interest in education and closely watched his schools. Here is an extract from his diary in March 1852:

'At 9 o'clock I employed, as I often do, the telescope to see the children enter school, which they usually do to a second, and rarely indeed is it that one or two are as many seconds beyond the proper time. One boy was about 3 seconds late . . . but it turned out that he had been hindered by an elder boy employed at the Washing Floors, and who is to come to the offices on Wednesday to be reprimanded.'

Just as many buildings in the remaining villages can be identified as traces of this once-great industry, so is the landscape scarred with evidence of the past mining, dressing and smelting. And there are traces of old pack horse tracks, and earthworks for the many railways which at one time have crossed the moors. The roads have survived, but the railways and pack horse tracks are now almost lost. The scattered settlements are mostly re-used as additional farm buildings or weekend cottages and in the villages themselves the community has shrunk. Nevertheless sufficient remains in the landscape, especially for the seeing eye, for us to discern a great deal. And the kind of documents already quoted, and many more to be found in libraries and archives, can bring those remains back to life.

Unfortunately there are very few people left alive today who can remember anything of this past great industry, since it virtually died seventy or more years ago. Recent years, however, have seen a new development in the dales, for fluorspar, once a waste product from the lead mines, is now required in large quantities as a flux for the steel industry. This means that not only have the old waste heaps recently been thoroughly worked over, but quite a number of mines are now being re-opened. Ironically lead is again being produced, but this time as a by-product.

5 Country Cottages

During the years of the Roman occupation, many buildings in the North were constructed of stone—that most plentiful raw material of the region—and their ruins have stood for almost two thousand years, though generally robbed down to their foundations in more recent times. Most of the northern Roman stone buildings were for defensive and allied puposes such as forts, granaries, bathhouses and the Wall itself. And in the centuries following the Roman occupation, stone continued to be used almost solely for defensive or ecclesiastical buildings by the Anglo-Saxons, the Danes and the Normans. Therefore, except for such buildings, and their burials and the monuments, we have little tangible evidence of how these people lived, though we can often trace the whereabouts of their settlements by their place-names which have persisted over many centuries. However, it is reasonable to suppose that clay and wood were the common cottage building materials they used. They are materials which leave little for even the archaeologist to observe, particularly when house replacements occur over centuries on the same site. Indeed excavations of various early occupied sites generally show frequent rebuilds on each house site. This suggests that the cottages did not have a very long life before repair or complete replacement became necessary, and it is quite likely that many existing seventeenth-century stone cottages represent the last of a whole series of cottages on that site, though probably the first to be built there in stone.

But before coming to the seventeeth-century, we must recall those earlier disturbed centuries when the peoples of the Border lived in fear of the loss of their lives or their cattle. The most northerly parts of our region had a history different in many respects from that of the rest of England and this difference is reflected in the nature of some of their domestic buildings. Best known are probably the 'pele-towers'. Although these are also found a little further south, they are particularly typical of the Border country and an impressive number of them stretch south-westwards across Northumberland as safeguards against the marauding Scots.

A further scatter can be traced through County Durham and one of the most southerly ones is a well-preserved example at Rokeby, south of Barnard Castle. Pele towers (the name comes from the Latin word *pilum,* a stake and hence a palisade) are not easily dated. Some probably date from as early as the thirteenth century and they seem to have gone on being built with very little change until the accession of James I in 1603 united, to some degree, the two Crowns of Scotland and England. In 1541 a list of all the Castles of Northumberland was made, containing over a hundred, and the majority of these are pele towers. These heavily constructed towers are mostly oblong in plan with a tunnel-vaulted ground floor and one, two, or three upper storeys connected by a spiral staircase built into the wall at one corner. Although pele towers have been known and written about for many years, a less-known type of fortified house, also peculiar to the region, has only recently been described—the bastle house. These buildings are of interest on several counts. They were fortified or at least defensible farmhouses, they seem to be peculiar to a fairly narrow strip of country running through Northumberland and parts of Cumberland and they are probably the only farmhouses in the British Isles which, in one building, accommodate animals on the ground floor and human beings on an upper floor. This is a building style not uncommon in the Alps, but very rare in the British Isles.

The typical bastle is rectangular in plan, with external dimensions of about thirty-five feet by twenty-five feet and is of two storeys with quite steeply pitched gables. The walls are built of stone, frequently in large blocks of irregular shape and and the walls are about four feet thick at ground level, thinning to about three feet six inches at first floor level. There is generally only one entrance into the ground floor, frequently set in the middle of one of the gable walls. This is a narrow opening, generally not more than two feet six inches wide, but widening as one enters to about three feet six inches. The upper floor is entered through a doorway similar to the low one, but at first floor level. In all surviving bastles the approach to this doorway is now by an external stone staircase, but since this can be seen not to be bonded to the main wall, one may assume it to be a replacement, probably of a moveable wooden ladder.

Bastles can, for the most part, be dated to a period from about the middle of the sixteenth century to the middle of the seventeenth century. Their chief distinction from the better known pele tower is largely one of size. The pele tower was smaller in area but taller and better built and was generally meant to provide refuge for the lord and his retinue, whereas the rest of the local population sheltered themselves and their beasts in the nearby 'barmkin' or walled forecourt when danger threatened. On the other hand a bastle is intended as a full defence for a single

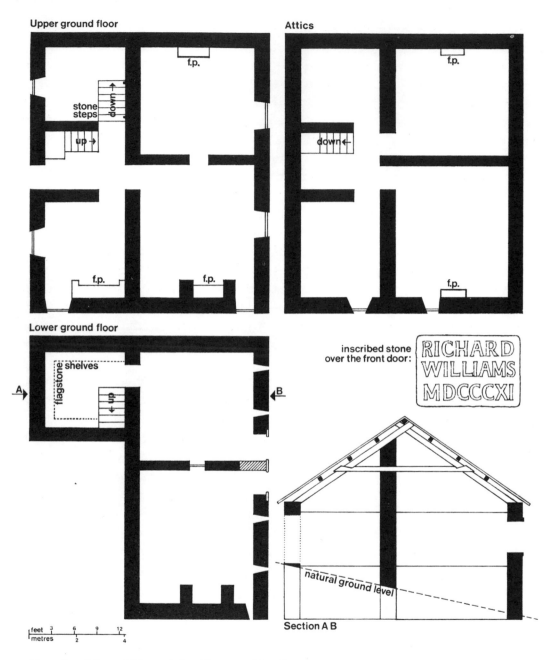

Upper ground floor

f.p.

stone
steps

down

up →

f.p.   f.p.

Attics

f.p.

down ←

f.p.

Lower ground floor

flagstone   shelves

A ►

up

◄ B

inscribed stone
over the front door:

RICHARD
WILLIAMS
MDCCCXI

natural ground level

Section A B

feet   3   6   9   12
metres   2   4

Crooks Altar, Weardale, County Durham

Fig. 12.   House above; cow house below ! See plate 27.

man and his family; he would drive his cattle into the ground floor space and shelter above. Hence a bastle is not merely a poor man's tower; it is a poor man's tower and a barmkin in one.

Finally it is interesting to observe that, once the style of the bastle house had been established, the design continued to be used in the northern region for two centuries or so after there was any real need for any such stout protection. For example a house has been recorded in Weardale (Crooks Altar) which was built as late as 1811, according to its dated door-head, yet this was built into a hillside with accommodation for cattle below and for the family above. One may assume that this was built along the old style, not as a response to the need for protection, but simply because it was the old way. Moreover the warmth from the cattle below was doubtless communicated to the human beings above and this could well have helped to perpetuate the practice of living above the byre. Such buildings are traditional in the fullest sense of the word.

Although the only mediaeval buildings to be found in the region's country districts are of stone, in the towns occasional mediaeval timber buildings can still be found. This is probably because changes in fashions and new styles have always affected towns more than the countryside. Newcastle, for example, still retains a fine timber frontage near the Swing Bridge and the overhanging fronts down Silver Street in Durham indicate structures hidden under later brickwork and stucco. A good indication of timber structure can be seen on the exposed gable of a house near the bottom of South Street in Durham, and in Barnard Castle mediaeval timbers were uncovered during demolition in 1960 at the junction of Bridgegate and the Bank. These latter houses had every appearance of being non-descript nineteenth-century dwellings, but as the outer walls fell away, 'half timbering' was exposed, indicating that a form of 'modernisation' had taken place last century. Perhaps other examples are still concealed.

Although timber was not used for external structures in the country districts of the North-East during the mediaeval period, it was of course used for internal features such as roof trusses and panelling and for window frames and doors. Several examples of these are preserved. Many early roof trusses doubtless wait to be discovered, hidden by later ceilings and sometimes a steep pitched roof can indicate what are known as 'upper-crucks'—curved pairs of timbers built into the upper walls and curving up to meet at the ridge and thus support a narrow high roof. Cruck timbers are curved pairs of timbers which stand, on stone footings, the width of a room apart, and are joined together at the ridge. The weight of the roof, in a cruck cottage, is thus carried directly to the ground and the sidewalls do not support the roof and could be as light as desired. Few cruck cottages are known in the north, though they certainly have existed at some time.

Upper-crucks are of curved timbers similar to those of crucks, but instead of springing from ground level, they are built into the upper part of the side walls thus permitting the cottages to be built two storeys high. These probably date from the sixteenth or seventeenth centuries and a number of examples can still be seen. Quite frequently, if one explores the loft of a steep-roofed cottage, one will find that it has upper cruck roof timbers. Good examples have been recorded in ruined buildings at Hunderthwaite near Romaldkirk in Upper Teesdale, and at Escomb just across the road from the Saxon Church.

As we have seen, few stone cottages are to be found in the north earlier than the seventeenth century, though a number of manor houses and ecclesiastical dwellings such as East Deanery at St Andrew Auckland are appreciably earlier. East Deanery, until recently a farm and now unfortunately semi-derelict, was built on land given by Bishop Bek in 1291. One ground floor room is tunnel-vaulted and another has stout cambered beams and joists, whilst externally there are two-light windows, now somewhat decayed in appearance.

A few fine seventeenth century-farmhouses and others somewhat grander and a little earlier are still to be seen. Good examples are Gainford Hall (1603) and Howden Hall (c. 1600), and also that attractive sixteenth century town house in Barnard Castle known as Blagroves. Not entirely surprisingly, in view of the proximity of the restless Border country, there are more seventeenth-century country farmhouses to be found in Durham than Northumberland, but we even have to seek for these, and several good examples have been lost in recent years.

Plain though not unattractive seventeenth-century cottages still stand away from the main road, for example at Blackton in Baldersdale, off upper Teesdale and on this farm the Iceton family has probably spent most of the last three centuries, though moving out of the house into a more spacious one built nearby last century. Unfortunately the coming of the Balderhead reservoir took away most of the sheep-run and William Iceton decided to move away from his family home four or five years ago. The Blackton example is typical of many such Dales farmhouses, of single storey, with byre and house under one long stone-flagged roof. Unfortunately, apart from the stone-mullioned windows and dated doorhead few original details remain. Another stone building of this date, perhaps a little grander, was discovered a few years ago in the final stages of decay, but with traces of a fine stone arched fireplace. This, at Newfield near Willington, not only had had a large arched fireplace, but to each side of this had been a narrower arched recess; that on the left (nearer the house front) was probably used for a cupboard and through the other came the doorway from the cross passage behind the fireplace—a common northern plan.

A very attractive though tiny seventeenth-century cottage was recently dis-covered in a rather unlikely spot, less than three miles from Consett. Here at about 850 feet OD stands Fell Close cottage now with a sheet iron roof and much altered front wall, but with original first floor with rather plain chamfered beams and a fine studded oak door in the west gable. The roof was clearly originally thatched with heather and the ruined west porch still carries scraps of heather.

Heather thatch must often have been used in country districts. Due to their relatively short life few of these thatches have survived, though several have been recorded in the last fifteen years from such places as Bowes, Upper Teesdale, Weardale and near Stocksfield (Tynedale). The local name for heather thatch was 'black thack' and once one has seen the remains of a heather thatch this description is appreciated. The technique as recounted by Jack Peart of Weardale was messy but fairly long lasting. The rafters were laid close together and heather pulled up in large tufts—roots and all, was nailed to the timbers. Once the roof had been covered wet peat was liberally applied, followed by a further layer of heather which was placed roots uppermost. This was held in place by pegs and more peat applied. Thus a very heavy roof cover was built up which gradually consolidated to well over a foot in thickness.

To look further backwards in time, northern roofing materials must be in part conjectural when we are dealing with the mediaeval period, but probably heavy flagstones were often used and certainly many examples still exist from the seven-teenth century. Later, pantiles became very popular, with the added advantage of being lighter and requiring less timberwork in the roof. They seem to have had a fairly long period of popularity and are said to have first been imported from the Lowlands as a form of high-grade ballast. However brick and tile kilns of the eighteenth and nineteenth centuries are to be found in many parts of southern and central Northumberland, indicating that eventually a healthy local production developed. The arrival of the railway system in the mid-nineteenth century made possible the cheap import of the ubiquitous Welsh blue slate and the final loss of distinctive regional roofing.

Several of the cottages described and illustrated here have been destroyed over the past two decades or so, and others have been 'modernised', so that it is now difficult to find cottages in any recognisably early state. The gradual depopulation of the Dales, which began in the second half of last century, probably reached the worst point in the early years after the second world war. Subsequently the economic and social changes of the sixties, which led to so many families having a

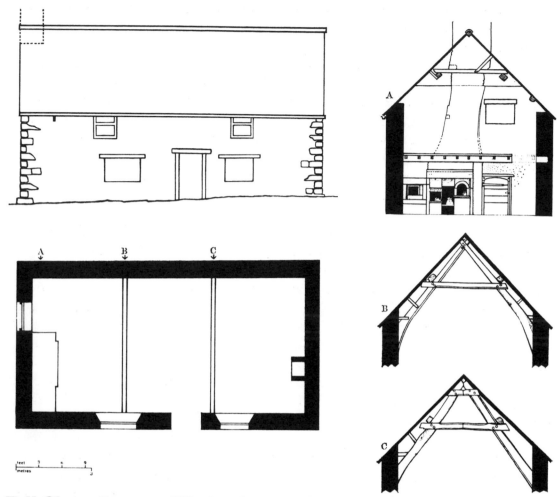

Fell Close Cottage, Waskerley, Co. Durham

Peter Brears Dip AD, AMA

Fig. 13a and b. Once a heather-thatched cottage, near Consett.
Although now used as a cattle shelter, this building retains several original and early features. See plate 30.

'country cottage', seemed at first to be saving the deserted houses from final decay, but recent legislation which encouraged building 'improvements' has resulted in inappropriate doors and windows, new roofs often with dormers and the complete destruction of internal details such as panelling and fireplaces. It is ironical that building regulations designed to maintain healthy living conditions, linked to grants intended to improve old property, should have so completely and irreparably damaged this aspect of the countryside. Grants were only payable for improvements which satisfied building regulations and these latter specified minimum window sizes for a given floor area. Thus the fenestration of most cottages—one of their most visually attractive and original features—was destroyed at a stroke.

Nevertheless there may still be one or two 'unimproved' cottages lying semi-derelict and if, by having described some original features, the writer has interested his readers in the genuine rather than the supposed 'antique' in such matters as stonework, woodwork, windows and roofs of the vernacular architecture of this region, then perhaps a few remaining examples will be properly conserved and preserved.

6 Lowland Farms and Villages

A casual drive through the older parts of the Northumberland and Durham coalfield, or a glance at a map of that area will suggest that the old mining settlements north of the Tyne, in Northumberland, tend to be of a straggling ribbon development, whereas south of the Tyne in Durham they tend to be more clustered. Following this, closer observation of many Durham mining village plans will suggest that the nineteenth and twentieth century miners' houses have clustered around much earlier villages. Ferryhill (fig. 14) and Trimdon are two very good and clear examples.

If we now look for these older village plans we shall find to our surprise that a good many (perhaps fifty or more) show a remarkable similarity. They tend to be long and narrow, sometimes with an elongated central green (such as Staindrop), sometimes just a wide central street and mostly roughly oriented east-west. Looking at a larger scale map it becomes clear that many of the houses fronting on to the street or green have gardens or yards running back quite a long distance and quite often there is a back lane (or series of back lanes) running almost round the whole village. Of course much of this detail is missing in many of the villages, but sufficient indications are generally there for one to recognise these similarities in village after village in East Durham. They have been described as 'green villages' and a convincing argument has recently been put forward for suggesting that many of them were deliberately planned and laid out in a regular way in the twelfth or early thirteenth century. It seems to be significant that these villages lie within the lands of the Prince Bishops of Durham and two pressures of the day may well have played a large part in the resultant planning. On the one hand there was a steady pressure from land-hungry peasants which led towards the expansion of old settlements and the creation of new ones. And on the other hand would be the financial needs of the great landholders on whose estates the villages were situated.

One needs also to recall that shortly after William of Normandy's conquest of England his armies were sent north to repress rebellion. This 'Harrying of the

North' resulted in a large area of waste-land which persisted for two generations or more. It is worth reading Symeon of Durham's description:

'In consequence of the Normans having plundered . . . principally Northumbria and the adjacent provinces, so great a famine prevailed that men, compelled by hunger, devoured human flesh, that of horses, dogs and cats, and whatever custom abhors. . . . Meanwhile, the land being thus deprived of anyone to cultivate it for nine years, an extensive solitude prevailed all round. There was no village inhabited between York and Durham; they became lurking places for wild beast and robbers, and were a great dread to travellers.'

Scarcely had those royal troops been withdrawn than Malcolm, King of Scotland, penetrated into Durham at the head of a marauding army, and in 1080, following the slaying of Walcher, bishop of Durham, in Gateshead, the area was again ravaged by Norman armies.

After such a sequence of devastating events it is not surprising that resettlement was an ordered and fairly systematic development of the land, rather than a haphazard re-occupation of old settlements. The wastes provided opportunities to landlords to reorganise and re-plan, and as one may perhaps expect, this seems to have taken place particularly in the south and east of Durham, where the land was good for corn and cattle.

It is not easy to point to any one village as being an ideal example of this kind of planning, since all have undergone many changes over the centuries and especially in the last hundred and fifty years, but occasionally it has been possible to find early maps of some of these villages and Fig. 14 is based on this kind of information. A search of many of these villages in their present-day form enables one to discern, here and there, some of these early features and this can be an exciting and rewarding pastime. Even today, for example, Ferryhill still holds glimpses of its early mediaeval shape, overlain as it is by the extensive housing of the early years of this century. It was constructed as the adjoininng Dean and Chapter Colliery was opened.

It is particularly interesting to observe the shape of the tofts in Fig. 14: those strips of land to the rear of each house, for these can often be identified even today from aerial photographs, and sometimes they can still be seen on the ground. Not only are they generally of a common length in each village, supporting the suggestion of a planned layout, but it can often be shown that each cottage had an equal frontage on to the village green. Look, for example, at the plan of Byers Green, a little village about three miles north of Bishop Auckland. The toft frontages on the west side of the village seem to be in the ratios 2 : 1 : 2 : 2 : 1 : 1 : 3

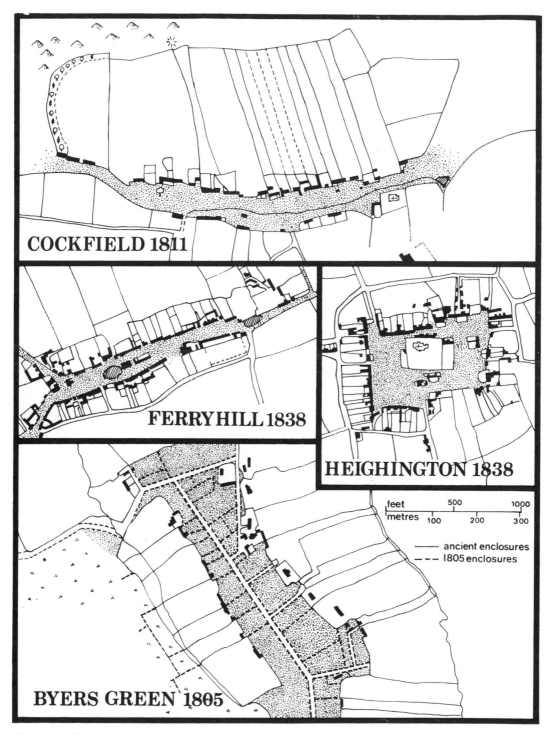

COCKFIELD 1811

FERRYHILL 1838

HEIGHINGTON 1838

BYERS GREEN 1805

feet   500   1000
metres   100   200   300

—— ancient enclosures
- - - 1805 enclosures

Fig. 14. *Durham green villages.*
These examples are illustrated from old plans and are based on a very useful paper by Dr Brian Roberts published in Mediaeval Archaeology, 1972.

and the actual measurements could have been based on the old standard rod of 16½ feet (5.03 m), the total street frontage being about ninety-six rods or twelve eight-rod units. (Perhaps many readers will recall the 'rod, pole or perch' of long-gone schooldays!)

Now all this mathematical juggling may seem a long way from my suggestion of a Sunday afternoon picnic and ramble, but it should help to stress some of the evidence upon which the theory has been based that these are early examples of planned villages.

As has already been mentioned, many country cottages which look old are often merely the latest of a whole series of cottages built roughly on the same site—and this holds good for these villages just as it does for isolated buildings. Many of the older houses to be seen in these Durham villages such as Staindrop or Heighington or Middridge, appear to have been built in the eighteenth century, or occasionally, the seventeenth century, and this may well be so. They were modernised or completely rebuilt at that time but, as can now be seen, they stand on or adjoining foundations which were begun eight centuries or more ago; and we can almost see the landlord's agent walking across the ground with his measuring rod, marking out the tofts and allocating the land.

Of course there are many other kinds of rural settlements in the North-East in addition to these 'green villages'. There are, for example, fishing villages such as Boulmer and small rural ports such as Craster and Beadnell; there are one or two eighteenth-century planned villages of which Blanchland is an outstanding example and there are many nineteenth-century mining villages: some of the mechanical grid design such as Easington Colliery, some of ribbon development such as Easington Lane, and others of square plan such as Quebec and Esh Winning. All these colliery villages are usually closely associated with the pit which brought them into being and have clusters of allotments, with pigeon crees and garden huts. A few have grown into towns such as Ashington and Consett and others have disappeared completely, having been demolished when their period of usefulness was ended. Bewicke Main near Lamesley in County Durham is a well-documented example of a recent 'lost village' and another is Page Bank which lay between Brancepeth and Spennymoor. There have, of course, been several much older villages also 'lost' in the North-East, though what are referred to in the historian's jargon as DMV's (or deserted mediaeval villages), are not so common here as in the midlands.

And what of the farming which was the prime function of almost all except the pit villages? In the first place it must be emphasised that over most of our area the mediaeval system of agriculture was closer to the Scottish *runrig* than to the open—

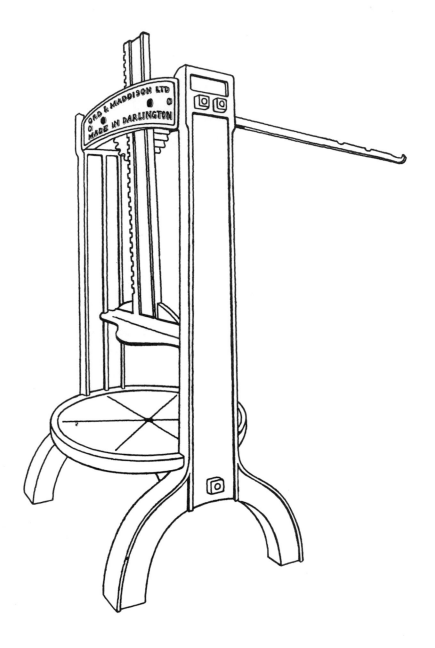

Fig. 15. Cast-iron cheese press.
These were once very common, for every farmhouse would have one or more. The makers of this example,
Ord and Maddison of Darlington, were well-known iron-founders, making all kinds of agricultural
implements.

or three-field system of the English lowlands. Occasionally the latter was found in the North-East, as for example at Bishop Auckland, but elsewhere early cultivation was such that two fields were used—the *outfield* and the *infield*. The infield received all the manure and was continuously cultivated until it was exhausted. It was then fallowed whilst the outfield was temporarily reclaimed from the surrounding waste. The outfield was ploughed and sown for one year and then left for a long time to recover. An Enclosure Act of 1840 for Gunnerton in North Tynedale clearly specifies the 'ingrounds' and the 'outgrounds' and another, of 1814, distinguishes at Gateshead between the 'townfields' and 'other commonable lands and grounds'.

This runrig system of agriculture was not only encouraged by the physical conditions of relief, soil and climate, but can be seen in some parts as the strength of the British element in society and the persistence of British custom. ('British' is being used here in the sense of the earlier occupants of the North-East, who later fused with the Anglian and Norse immigrants.) These two possible reasons for the continuance of the runrig system—physical conditions and persistence of custom—can be seen as complementary, for the physical conditions of farming in the north tended to preserve the pastoral runrig system as practised by the British. On the other hand conditions were easier in the south of Durham and the area of the so-called 'Northallerton gate' where connection was provided with the English lowlands, and here one finds the open-field system being adopted.

Over subsequent centuries the land was gradually enclosed, though it is difficult to be precise about this process since there is little if any contemporary evidence preserved. But by 1800 the lowlands of Northumberland and Durham had been almost entirely enclosed, mostly by quick hedges and, at higher levels, by stone walls. The reporters to the Board of Agriculture in 1794, for example, noted that the Glendale district of north Northumberland, then being enclosed, was exceptional among the farmlands of Northumberland, and in the bishopric of Durham in 1726 it was estimated that already nine parts in ten were enclosed.

The period of 1750 to 1850 was a time of growth, for the dramatic changes in industry and the considerable population increase encouraged an increase in food production and this in turn led to many agricultural improvements. The threshing machine and the often-associated gin-gan are mentioned in chapter 7, as being one such improvement, which diffused through the region from Scotland. But other improvements took place within the North-East, and made their mark throughout the country. The Durham Ox, for example, is well-known as a massive beast which was the result of careful selective breeding, particularly by the brothers Charles and Robert Colling who lived near Darlington. They won fame with their Durham

Shorthorn cattle and the famous Ox was taken round the country to be exhibited at Agricultural Shows.

John Bailey gives a vivid description of the Ox in his *Agriculture of Durham*. He says: 'At five years old he was not only covered thick with fat . . ., but his whole carcase in a manner loaded with it, and was then thought to be so wonderful an animal, and so far exceeding whatever had been seen before, that he was purchased to be exhibited . . . in February 1801, for £140. At this time his live weight was 216 stones. . . He was travelled for six years through the principal parts of England and Scotland and in Oxford, on February 19th 1807 . . . the ox by accident dislocated his hip bone, and continued in that state until 15th April when he was obliged to be killed'. By that time the beast had lost weight by being ill for so long, yet his carcase then weighed 188 stones. A year earlier his live weight was recorded as 270 stones. Today we would not place such emphasis on mere weight, a large part of which was—to us—unnecessary fat, though one must remember that animal fat was at that time an essential product. Of the final dead weight of 188 stones almost 12 stones was recorded as 'tallow' and this would be used as the basis of candles and soap. The Durham Shorthorn breed still exists, though subsequent breeding has rather changed its direction. An important change was effected by Thomas Bates of Halton in the Tyne Valley and later of Kirklevington. He developed the milking strain and it is as the Dairy Shorthorn that we recognise the breed today.

Another northern animal bred during the years around 1800 was a line of sheep produced by two brothers, Matthew and George Culley, who farmed at Fenton in north Northumberland. In 1762 and 1763 they visited Robert Bakewell to see his famous New Leicester breed of sheep and then returned home to cross this with their native Teeswater sheep, giving the Border Leicester breed.

A manuscript preserved among the Northumberland County Archives describes one of the Culley's sheep of 1786. Its girth was 4 feet 8½ inches and 'his Mutton was of the most Beautiful bright Colour, and fine Grain marbled with fat and lean. . . . This Breed of Sheep has a greater quantity of Mutton . . . than any other kind we know of. . . . It is this Nutritious kind that not only satisfies the hunger of our Manufacturers, at the cheapest rate, but enables them to make those Exertions in Labour, at which surrounding Nations may wonder, but cannot attain to.' Perhaps we ought, as a nation, to try improving the quality of our mutton once more!

In order to bring this record of agricultural experimentation in the north up to date, the experimental farm at Cockle Park in Northumberland should be mentioned. As long ago as 1797 Bailey and Culley, in their *General View of the Agricul-*

ture of Northumberland, recommended the setting up of 'a public farm which would not only be a school where youth might be instructed in agriculture, but even experienced farmers might often visit it with advantage, to learn the results of new experiments. . . .' This scheme was too far ahead of its time and it was not until 1836 that the Northumberland Agricultural Society was formed. Almost immediately after the Northumberland County Council was established in 1889 it took an interest in promoting agricultural education and gave financial help towards founding a Chair of Agriculture in the Durham College of Science (based at Newcastle). Soon the need for a demonstration farm was recognised and eventually Cockle Park Farm was established in 1896. As experimental work became more advanced, the institution became less useful for teaching purposes and in 1947 it passed into the sole control of the University and a County Farm Institute was set up at Kirkley Hall. At Cockle Park world-famous plots, laid down in 1896 by Professor Somerville, have been used to demonstrate the value of basic slag and other equally important experiments have been carried out here, demonstrating that the northern tradition of improved agricultural methods is still alive.

It is also interesting to observe, in this historical ebb and flow of improvements and changes, that the industrial growth of the second half of the nineteenth and first half of the twentieth centuries resulted in a loss of both farming land and quality of soil condition, for industrial pollution produced an acid pasture. Today, however, the position is again improving for the recent marked decline in atmospheric pollution is permitting a more productive sward to be grown. And over the past ten years some 1500 acres of derelict land have been reclaimed in Durham alone, and returned to agriculture.

One may even, perhaps smilingly, note that the horse is staging a comeback, though only on a minute scale. Yet there are still men who can handle a ploughing team, and masters who are prepared to keep a few horses; and if the price of fuel continues to rise then, as George House pointed out in a recent BBC programme, some of these proud horse-owners may prove to be the lucky ones, with a cheap and well-proven way of working their farms.

7 Oxen, Horses and Engines

Farmers have, at different times, used various sources of power; some may seem obvious such as the horse, others less so. Certainly when one is thinking of last century the horse immediately springs to mind. But in earlier centuries the ox was more generally used, indeed solely used in the field until later mediaeval times, when the introduction of the horse-collar made it practicable for that animal to pull heavy loads. Nevertheless the ox continued as a draught animal for a long time. George Culley writing on *Live Stock* in 1807 commented: 'Fewer oxen are used in the draught now than formerly.' He went on to refer to the fact that though oxen were slower than horses, they still had advantages when considering feeding, shoeing and harness, but 'above all, the conclusion (between an ox fatted for the shambles, after working three or four years, or indeed a lean ox sold to feed, and a horse sold to the dog-kennel) is so exceedingly striking that I presume most people . . . will agree to the drawing of oxen . . . wherein they *suit*; I use the expression *suit* because I would not be understood to think, as some people do, that oxen will answer as will horses in every kind of farming-work, but oxen will do several kinds of horse-work (such as ploughing, leading dung, corn etc.) equally as well as horses. I advance this opinion on several years of experience.' Culley, who farmed at Wooler in Northumberland then pointed out that he and his brother, in partnership at this time (i.e. 1807), employed about 150 oxen 'in the draught'.

By the end of the nineteenth century, however, the ox had virtually disappeared from northern fields, though as plate 32 shows, oxen continued to be used in some rather isolated areas probably until the beginning of the present century.

The pack horse, or 'gallowa' (Galloway pony) was used in the north for several centuries as a beast of burden since no collar was needed for this purpose, only a pack saddle, securely strapped to the animal's back. Until the construction of turnpike roads in the eighteenth century, roadways were so inadequate that loads could rarely be taken any great distance except by pack horse, and long trains of these small hardy animals would cross the roughest of country. However this practice died out too long ago for us to be able either to collect old photographs or verbal recollections and we have to examine the material remains to seek any insight into this method of transport.

Pack horse tracks can be traced on six inch maps of the northern moorland, sometimes described as 'Limer's gates'—along which the burdens of burnt lime would be carried from kilns in the limestone country. Another name to be found on maps is 'Lead gate', along which packs of lead were carried to the coast for export. The word 'gate' incidentally, is a northern dialect word for a way or a path (see Chapter 14). And whilst the pack-horse tracks are just discernible, the actual pack saddles are very few. The North of England Open Air Museum, at Beamish, has one wooden saddle which was rescued by Mr Lamb of Egglestone. He remembered his uncle once telling him of how the lead was brought down from the Egglestone smelt mills, on the backs of 'gallowas', to Barnard Castle, and thence to Darlington (where the old name Leadyard indicates the place where it was stored before being sold). The wooden saddles, his uncle had said, were kept in a little tumble-down building still called the saddle-house, so one day about twenty years ago he went to investigate and found a fragile object, illustrated here on page 47. The saddle-house has subsequently achieved formal recognition and is now a 'Listed Building' and one cannot help feeling how remarkable it is that this wooden saddle should have remained there untouched for half a century. There can be little doubt that had Mr Lamb not rescued it when he did, it would have suffered at the hands of youthful vandals before much longer, for the countryside is much more visited than it was only a quarter of a century ago.

Whilst the ox and, later the horse, provided the farm with draught power, such animals were of little use when rotary motion was required. Of little use, that is, until a new machine came into use - the horse-gin. This was a wooden contraption not unlike the children's roundabout seen at fairgrounds, into which were harnessed horses. The horses plodded around a circular path, rotating the 'gin' (short for *engine*) which, by means of gears, drove other machinery. Such gins had been used for centuries in mining and a book on this subject published in Germany in 1556 illustrated many such machines. However, on the farm where manpower was cheap and rotary motion not generally required, except for such simple processes as winding at the well or pumping, these rotary horse-powered machines were not used. But when, in 1788 Andrew Meikle produced the first successful threshing machine, the need for farm rotary power suddenly became much greater. The thresher spread quite rapidly from southern Scotland across north-eastern England and various ways of driving it were tried out. Small threshers were made which could be worked manually, by a winding-handle, but this must have been exhaust-

Fig. 16.   A Durham long-cart.
The long-cart is characteristically northern, but there are variations within the region. This one came from near Darlington.

Fig. 17.   A Northumberland long-cart.
The body is lighter and the shafts tend to be broader than they are thick, to allow for the sideways lurch of the Clydesdale horse.

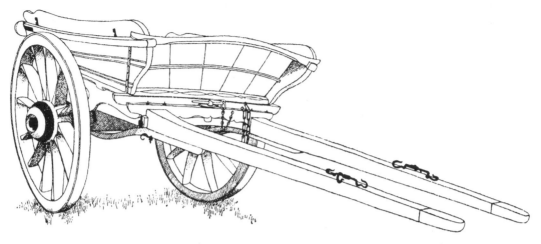

Fig. 18. *A Hexhamshire coup-cart.*
This short bodied cart comes from near Hexham and the entire body only rests on the axle. Thus on very rough ground the cart-body tips off instead of injuring the horse. Probably made by Symms of Newton near Stocksfield.

Fig. 19. *A rolley.*
Another northern vehicle, but used on the road rather than the fields. This can be deduced from the heavy springing. It would probably be used to take goods to market. Built by Coates of Stockton.

ing work especially with the designs then available. So it is not surprising that the horse-gin was quickly adapted for this purpose. Smeaton, the great mechanical innovator of the late eighteenth century, had used such gins to drive some of the industrial concerns he designed and the simple horse-gin seems to have proved eminently successful on northern farms. So by 1800 horse-gins were beginning to be constructed across Northumberland and Durham. They were generally constructed inside single-storey buildings attached to the barn in which the thresher could be erected. Almost, invariably this building can be seen to have been added to the farm, not unnaturally, since very few farms were being built in the early nineteenth century. So far only one farm has been discovered in the North-East which was built in its entirety between 1810 and 1813 and which included a 'horse-walk' as an original and integral part of the buildings. This is Cordilleras Farm near Marske in North Yorkshire. It was observed by Mrs Vera Chapman who has written a full description of this farm and its development.

These 'horse-walks' are given a variety of dialect names, that in Northumberland being *gin-gan*. 'Gin' is short for *engine* and 'gan' comes from the dialect word *to go*. ('Gannin along the Scotswood Road, to see the Blaydon Races', is the refrain of a popular Tyneside song from the music halls of last century.)

Not only do these buildings have a variety of names, but they are found in a variety of shapes and materials. The typical Northumberland one is circular, with circular stone columns and a beautifully conical slated roof. Durham ones tend to be hexagonal, with square pillars and North Yorkshire ones are hexagonal or square, with pantiled roofs.

Some time ago I talked to an elderly farmer not far from Croft, just south of Darlington—an area thick with 'wheelhouses' as they tend to be called round there. He recollected working in the building, where four horses were employed. Usually they could plod around without too much difficulty once they had got the machine turning and the man up in the threshing stead would shout down when there was no more corn to be threshed. (There is usually a little door or window between the thresher and the interior of the wheelhouse.) 'Sometimes', he went on, 'we would put a young horse in, to break it in. It would kick and scream, but it had to go round when the other horses went. Terrible it was, blood and sweat and shit all over—but it worked!'

Although the horse was seized upon to provide rotary power for Meikle's thresher there had of course long been other, inanimate sources of rotary power. The windmill and the watermill have been common features of the northern landscape as they have elsewhere in the country. Nowadays these visible remains are few, but some which are characteristically northern in character can still be seen. The wooden post-mill, so common in southern and midland England, has been rarer if not completely absent in the north. Instead we have had stone or brick towers capped with a rotatable wooden structure supporting the sails and designed to turn these into the wind. A few such towers are still preserved, for

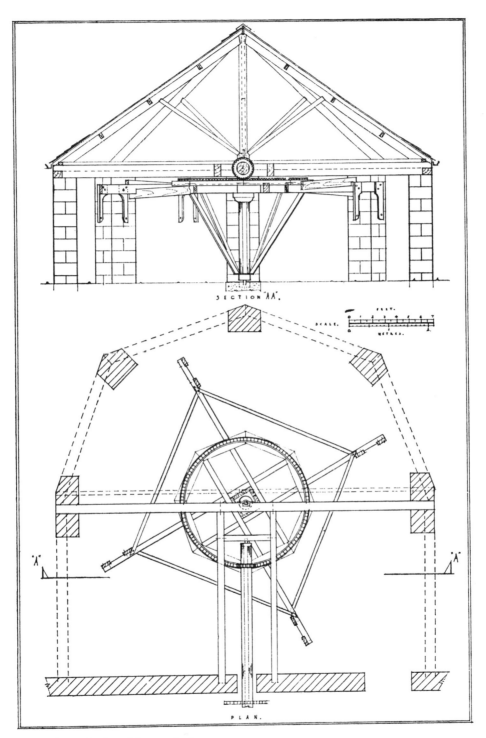

SECTION "AA".

SCALE.

FEET.

METRES.

PLAN.

Fig. 20.   An agricultural horse wheel.
This four-horse wheel is preserved at Beamish, North of England Open Air Museum and came
from near Ponteland, Northumberland.

example Woodhorn Mill near Ashington, Billy Mill near North Shields, one at Elswick and another nearby at Hart, west of Hartlepool and a good example is partially restored at Fulwell, north of Sunderland. Old prints of Newcastle show the surrounding countryside dotted with such mills, some of which were once used to pump water out of the coal mines.

Thus, when the threshing machine became a practical proposition, around 1800, one obvious power source was the windmill and a few farms in Northumberland (for example at Chollerton near Hexham) still have surviving stone towers possibly built for this purpose, though doubtless also used for flour-grinding.

Whilst some threshers were being built on Northumbrian farms using wind for power, more were being constructed to be driven by water. For water power has for centuries been a traditional countryside source of power. It has an advantage over windpower in that it can, to a limited extent, be stored thus permitting greater freedom to the user. Hundreds of watermills are to be found in the North-East, as of course they are in hilly districts throughout the country, on farms and in villages. However there seems to be an 'upland' type of water-powered flour mill found generally in the Pennines and northern England which differs in its mechanical and building design from otherwise similar watermills in southern and lowland England. Kenneth Major, an authority on watermills, points out that upland mills are usually smaller, with little storage space. Their wheels are generally overshot or high-breast shot (that is to say the water is led to the very top of the wheel, or to a high side point, say one o'clock or two o'clock in position). These water wheels are generally large in diameter though probably only driving two pairs of stones. In the upland mill, too, other processes than flour grinding may have been carried on, such as the drying of wet grain in kilns, the production of roast oatmeal in other kilns and the production of pearl barley in rotating 'polishers'.

Water has often been led to these mills along a 'leat' constructed along and above the river bed or round a hillside, in order to bring the water to the top of the wheel. From the foot of the wheel the water could then run back to the river. These leats are generally excavated or banked earthworks though they terminate in a wooden trough close by the wheel. Occasionally, as at Riding Mill in south Northumberland, the wooden leat or launder has run for a much longer distance on the top of a stone wall or wooden trestle. Sometimes the leat system leads directly away from the riverside though mostly a small dam across the river helps to fill the leat. Older six inch maps of Northumberland (less so in County Durham) show farms with small dams uphill from the buildings, fed by a small stream. These were obviously built to provide a source of power for a threshing machine and can therefore be dated to between about 1800 and 1850. By this latter date stationary steam engines were being built and the older, rural, sources of power were being superseded.

Although the steam engine was first invented in the early 1700s, and greatly improved throughout the eighteenth century, it long remained a large and expensive machine to build and operate, and it was not until about the middle of the last century that the stationary steam engine had been sufficiently developed to be an economic proposition on a farm. Thus one finds farms in the North-East having chimneys built for this purpose, during the 1860s and 70s. Only one dated chimney has been found in the region and that is at Gilling West, near Richmond in North Yorkshire. It is built in brick and dated 1874. These farm steam engines were built to drive the stationary threshing machine, and so replaced horse-wheels, windmills and water mills. Not infrequently the farm buildings still include both gin-gan and chimney, indicating that modernisation took place probably in the 1870s. One such example is Beamish Home Farm on the site of the North of England Open Air Museum, another is at Fourstones near Hexham. At Chollerton, mentioned above, the group of farm buildings includes both stone windmill tower and brick chimney.

By the end of the nineteenth century the steam traction engine had made the stationary engine unnecessary and threshing was done by this means. The engine pulled a mobile threshing machine thus relieving the farmer of the need to build and own his own stationary one. Many people alive today remember threshing time (see plate 36), when the traction engine stood throbbing in the farm yard, driving the thresher by means of a long belt. But the Second World War brought yet another change: the 'combine harvester' was imported from the United States. Several of these came into the North-East in the 1940s and were much prized by their owners. So much so that, when not many years ago the North of England Open Air Museum was offered an early 'combine', the farmer said: 'For goodness sake come and collect it quickly so that I can get my new machine under cover!' For his elderly father still prized the old machine so much that he insisted upon it occupying valuable shed space, to the exclusion of a much newer machine.

8 River, Coast and Sea

The big river ports of the North-East have tended to be used for trade rather than fishing and the high cliffs of the Durham coastline have discouraged much coastal development there. Moreover, the size and strength of Newcastle has, throughout several centuries, tended to restrict the growth of other port facilities. There is a long history of disagreement between Newcastle and the Shields and similarly with Sunderland. In fact it was not until the tremendous nineteenth-century industrialisation that these ports could flourish freely, unhindered by the restrictive practices of Newcastle.

Hence although there have been large fishing fleets working from, for example, Shields on the Tyne and Whitby to the south, the major occupation of many of these north-eastern ports has been the shipment of coal. And although Newcastle prospered on its coal trade, admirably sited among readily accessible coal seams, other ports expanded this trade last century: ports such as Amble, Blyth, Sunderland and Stockton. Moreover two ports were constructed specifically for this purpose: Seaton Sluice in south Northumberland and Seaham Harbour in County Durham. Seaton Sluice has now shrunk back to a tiny pleasure harbour, but around two centuries ago when a large glass-bottle works stood by the waterside, coal was brought from the nearby coal mines of the Delaval family for export, and that same family constructed a new 'cut' through solid rock to provide a safe haven for the coastal shipping. Sufficient time has passed for one to be able to view the slight remains with sadness and interest, rather than the sorrow and depression with which one looks at the untidy dereliction of more recent industrial decay.

Seaham Harbour, on the other hand, continues to be relatively active and is still linked with a coal mine, though much of the adjoining town has lost the splendour with which Lord Londonderry sought to endow it, when he founded it in 1828. Even he was unable to complete the ambitious plans which he invited John Dobson of Newcastle to formulate, at the time when the harbour was constructed.

Other ports along this coast have also suffered a decline, such as Alnmouth at the mouth of the River Aln, which was once a thriving port, importing timber and guano and exporting grain. Jack Stewart, a retired fisherman recalls hearing of those days, last century, but when he was a boy (and he was born in 1889), all that had gone and there were only four fishing boats still catching haddock, a little cod and occasional plaice. At one time there were quite a number of these cobles, each manned by three men, but they became fewer as trawling developed and many of the fishermen had to return to the land. Jack Stewart and his father and brother worked one of the last of Alnmouth's cobles, fishing by five-hundred-yard-long lines each baited with about a thousand hooks. 'You baited the lines after they'd been used and shot—when the boat returned with the fish', said Jack Stewart. 'You started to bait the lines when you got back, but sometimes if the weather was too rough to go out, they might stand for a week, and then they all went bad and we had to clear them off and bait again'. Bait was mussels and in springtime they dug for lugworms. The mussels had to be brought from Boston or Morecambe, because there were none around Alnmouth, though sometimes they got limpets off the rocks.

The lines were shot over a smooth sandy bottom, about three to four miles out, and then raised perhaps half or three quarters of an hour later. An average catch for a coble would be about 60 stones, though exceptionally Jack Stewart remembers his father coming back with 109 stones, and the boat was only just above the waterline. As to selling the fish, he recalls that they used to send it in fish boxes by rail to Yorkshire and the Midland towns, but his grandmother told him how she had had a donkey with two creels, 'And she used sometimes to come back with no money, because it was all barter. The creels would be full of pieces of bacon, and butter and pieces of mutton and a few eggs or potatoes and cabbages—anything eatable, from the farmers who took her fish. She said she only used to get money at what she called the big houses—otherwise it was all barter.'

Now Alnmouth is little more than a quiet village by the sand dunes, though the old buildings which more than a century ago were big granaries holding the grain ready for export, can still be recognised—now used as the vicarage, as flats, and Prospect Place. 'And now', says Jack Stewart thinking of all those fishermen 'there's nobody left but me!'—and the guano storehouses and timber yards have all gone too.

Mention of timber recurs frequently in recollections of imports along the north-eastern coast, which was conveniently sited for the Scandinavian timber trade. It is still an important import to the Tyne, to the Wear and to Hartlepool where timber yards still dominate parts of the landscape, though much less so than fifty years ago, when stocks were large not only on account of the great use of timber for constructional purposes, but also because of the needs for lengthy seasoning. Many people still recollect an enormous fire which raged at Hartlepool for two or three days, in the 1920s, when many acres of stacked timber were destroyed. The pit-prop trade was then a considerable one and a variety of props in differing diameters and lengths were supplied to the region's coal mines to support the underground roofs of the working areas.

Along the quaysides of Amble, Blyth, Newcastle, Sunderland and Seaham Harbour large coal staithes were constructed in timber last century to carry coal trucks to the water's edge. From these, various spouts and chutes carried the coal down into the waiting colliers. A century earlier still, staithes had an additional function—that of storing the coal until the tide and demand were right. But these were further upstream on the Tyne, as near as possible to the mines. They were so far upstream in fact, that sea-going colliers could not penetrate and smaller *keels* carrying some twenty tons of coal were ferried downsteam by three or four men to the waiting colliers. That well-known song 'Weel may the keel row' reminds us of that time. Not a single example of a Newcastle keel remains, thought there is always the hope that one may eventually be rescued from the mud of the Tyne!

The coal staithes of last century were linked to the inland railway system and were ingeniously designed so that loaded coal trucks could be run, singly and under gravity, to the top of the spout and then returned also by gravity to a slightly lower track whence they could be collected by steam locomotive. Many elderly port workers remember the 'coffee pot' locomotives used at Seaham Harbour, so-called on account of their curious vertical boiler-layout. These coffee-pots were built in the 1870s and 80s by Head Wrightson of Stockton.

The Tyne was not the only river to be worked well upstream, for the Tees was penetrated as far as Stockton during the nineteenth century, for the export of coal. One only has to remember the most famous coal and passenger carrying railway, the 'Stockton and Darlington', to realise how important Stockton was at that time. Still earlier, during the eighteenth century, sailing ships had worked their slow way up the Tees, well beyond Stockton to Yarm. The attractive tall buildings along the riverside at the rear of that town are the remaining indication of the many warehouses which must have been busily occupied at that time. Daniel Defoe in his *Tour through the Whole Island of Great Britain*, published in 1725, mentions 'two good towns, Stockton and Yarum, towns of no great note—but what they obtain by the river and adjacent sea, but are greatly encreased of late years . . . for the shipping of lead, and butter from London'.

In later years Middlesbrough completely took over the shipping trade of the Tees, growing from four farmhouses in 1830—when the first planned development

RURAL POWER

48. *A Northumbrian horse-wheel house, known locally as a 'gin-gan'. This one, at Belsay, is a typical circular slated Northumbrian example. In this building horses, harnessed to a 'wheel', would produce power to drive a thresher built in the adjoining barn.*

49. *A photograph taken around 1900 of a 'breast-turned' water wheel at Cotherstone in upper Teesdale. The leat or wooden trough carrying the water from further upstream can be seen at the left.*

50. *A farm with a chimney near Berwick on Tweed. Buttery Hall Farm stood until recently near the A1 a few miles south of Berwick. The chimney carried smoke from a stationary steam engine (in the small square building to the immediate left of the chimney). The engine, probably built around 1860 or 1870, powered a stationary thresher in the barn beyond.*

51. *A stationary steam engine built by Gilkes and Wilson of Middlesbrough in 1858. This drove a thresher and other barn machinery at a farm at St Helen's Auckland until about 1909. It is now in the collections of the North of England Open Air Museum at Beamish in County Durham.*

52. *This finely built stone windmill tower is at Elwick, inland from Hartlepool. Stone-built towers of this kind have been more common in the North than the South, where wooden post-mills were more usual. Much of the machinery remains, though quite inaccessible, on the upper floors.*

53. *Tynemouth beach with the Plaza ballroom in the background.*

54. *The quayside at Whitby, about 1910.*

55. *Harbour scene, probably at North Shields. On the right is the supply cart of lamp oil.*

56. *Hartlepool at the beginning of the century, with paddle tug on the right.*

57. *Preparing fishing nets at Newbiggin-by-the-Sea, in the 1920s.*

58. *Lang Sall and Fat Bess — Holy Island fishwives.*

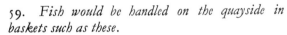
59. *Fish would be handled on the quayside in baskets such as these.*

60. *An old sea coal gatherer, about 1890 at Seaton Carew. Lumps of coal could be raked up on the beach and sold for a few coppers.*

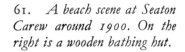
61. *A beach scene at Seaton Carew around 1900. On the right is a wooden bathing hut.*

62. *A fish-quay discussion, probably at North Shields.*

63. *A pause in the fish gutting at North Shields.*

64. *Packing the fish into barrels for long-distance sale from Newbiggin.*

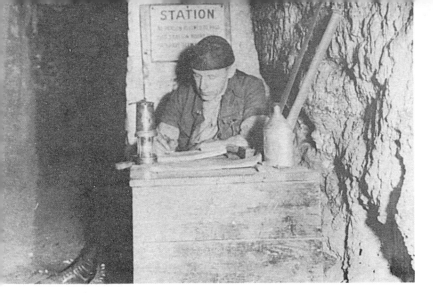

THE LIFE OF A COAL MINER

65. *The deputy at his kist, probably around 1920. The deputy is an underground foreman and his kist, or chest, is his 'office', where men are allocated their work. He is wearing a leather skull-cap worn at that time only by deputies; now replaced by toughened helmets for everyone underground.*

66. *Working at the coal face.*

67. *Below left: This man is kirving, or cutting out a deep notch along the lower edge of the coal seam so that it will drop cleanly when a shot is fired into it.*

68. *Below: Filling a tub from a coal conveyor. This is a relatively recent photograph since the man is wearing a helmet and electric cap lamp and the tub is an all-metal one.*

69. *Drilling a hole into the coal, in which a shot will then be placed and fired. A large twist drill can be used since coal is relatively soft. Ashington Colliery, Northumberland, 1911.*

70. *A fairly recent photograph of a pit pony at work underground. Very few pits now use ponies.*

71. *The underground stables at Greenside Colliery, County Durham.*

72. These ponies are being trained to work in a pit, at Taylor's Wood, near Consett, around 1920.

73. A group of pitmen at Woolley Colliery, Billy Row, near Crook, about 1900 in pit hoggers.

74. Coal picking at the screens, the place where the coal is brought at the top of the shaft. The coal was examined in this way, and pieces of shale or rock picked out. This task has now been replaced by 'washing'— a flotation process.

76. A group of shaft sinkers at Ludworth Colliery, 1930s. These men are wearing 'back-skins'—large leather sheets strapped over their shoulders, and their leather helmets also have long backflaps, to protect them from water falling in the shaft, whilst they are sinking (i.e. digging) the shaft.

75. Two shaft sinkers who were engaged in rescue work at the Stanley disaster, 1909.

COAL MINES, STAITHES AND COKING

77. *St Hilda Colliery, South Shields, about 1880. To the left are the headstock and screens. The coal wagons, locally known as 'black' or 'chaldron' wagons, originally held a chaldron of coal which weighed 53 cwt (about 2700 Kg).*

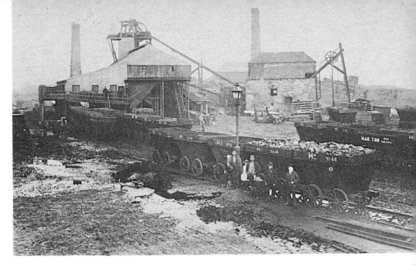

78. *Blue Bell Pit, Shiremoor, Northumberland, showing the headstock and screens.*

79. *Looking down Pelton self-acting incline. In the distance are three rails which divide towards the foreground, where the tracks come up over the 'humps'. A set of loaded trucks of coal was allowed to run down the slope and, by means of an attached rope, this weight brought back a set of empty trucks.*

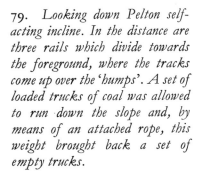

80. *Harton coal staithes, South Shields. Just to left of centre a coal truck is about to be lowered to the waiting collier, by means of a coal-drop. This, rather than a chute, was used last century since the coal was being handled in large pieces and every effort was made to reduce breakage.*

81. *A coal spout, or chute on the Wear, near Sunderland Bridge. The winch could lower the spout until it reached the moored collier.*

82. *The dock at Seaham Harbour, with coal staithes opposite and two paddle tugs at the right. The 'L' seen on the chaldron wagons stands for 'Londonderry'—since the nearby mines were owned by the Marquis of Londonderry.*

83. *A coal spout on the Wear, seen from above. Coal was discharged from the bottom of the coal truck into the opening and thence down to the spout.*

84. *A 'beehive' coke oven at Rowlands Gill. The white-hot coke is being 'quenched' by a jet of water, before being raked out.*

85. *Coke being lifted out of a 'beehive' coke oven by means of a long-handled rake. The weight is supported by a small swivelling crane.*

86. *Coke, after being lifted out of the coke oven, is swung round and tipped on to the 'bench', a platform from which it will be forked into rail trucks.*

87. *A set of by-product recovery vertical coke ovens at Crook, County Durham about 1890. These were an improvement on 'beehive' ovens, for not only could by-products such as benzole, tar, ammonia and gas be recovered, but the ovens could be discharged by machine. In the foreground is the steam-powered ram which pushed the coke out of the oven.*

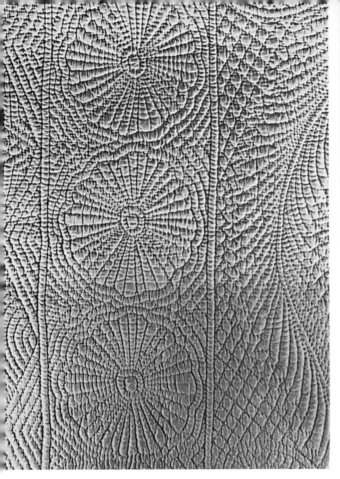

THE PITMAN AT HOME

89. *A quilt in ivory sateen made near Sunderland by a miner's wife, about 1890. Now in the Beamish collections.*

90. *A white cotton quilt, stamped or marked with an elaborate design typical of Allendale workers. It was made by Mrs Johnson of Dotland Park near Hexham, about 1898. See also plate 115.*

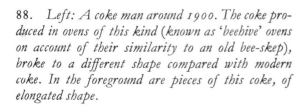

88. *Left: A coke man around 1900. The coke produced in ovens of this kind (known as 'beehive' ovens on account of their similarity to an old bee-skep), broke to a different shape compared with modern coke. In the foreground are pieces of this coke, of elongated shape.*

91. *Esh Winning from the air: taken by Professor McCord of the University of Newcastle upon Tyne in 1967, just before the village was demolished. Several north-eastern colliery villages were constructed to this general plan last century, with the colliery providing the last side of a square. The large area of water was the engine pond, to provide a regular supply of water for the steam engine.*

92. *A typical back street in a colliery village. Between each yard door can be seen two bricked-up openings. The higher one would be to take the coal, which would be tipped from a horse-drawn cart and then shovelled up into the coal-house. The lower opening was for the removal of nightsoil from the earth closet, or 'netty'.*

93. *The best decorated house of 1934 in Ryhope, near Sunderland. Unfortunately this photograph leaves several tantalising questions, and nothing further is known about it.*

took place, to a population of 7,600 in 1851. Ten years later the population had shot up to 19,000; in 1871 it was 39,500; and by 1901 it was 91,000. This development during the second half of the nineteenth century is unparalleled in England. Gladstone called the town in 1869 'the youngest child of England's enterprise, but, if an infant, an infant Hercules'. The iron ore discoveries in the adjoining Cleveland Hills in 1850 provided an enormous boost in the town's development, and the iron and steel industry boomed there, but has subsequently been replaced by the large-scale chemical works of the I.C.I. at Wilton to the south and at Billingham to the north.

Whilst such powerful growth was taking place at the southern end of our region, and Newcastle near the centre was almost past its prime, the small ports of Northumberland were quietly shrinking or dying. Berwick-on-Tweed had had quite an important trade in Tweed salmon two centuries ago, though not all was sent by sea very early in the eighteenth century, as Daniel Defoe (in 1725) observed: 'We receive every year at London a great quantity of salmon pickled or cured . . . which we call Newcastle salmon. Now when I came to Newcastle I . . . was surprised to find that there was no great quantity. . . . Upon enquiry I found that really this salmon, which we call Newcastle salmon, is taken as far off as the Tweed and is brought by land on horses to Shields, where it is cured and pickled . . . so that it ought to be called Berwick salmon, not Newcastle.'

Salmon fishing was—and to some extent still is—done from small cobles. Larger examples are found nearer the mouth, and smaller ones up-river. A few may still be seen for example, not far from the Union Bridge. They are flat-bottomed, square-sterned, clinker-built open boats from 16 to 22 feet in length, with a pronounced sheer forward, and having an open space aft for stowing the nets.

It was probably during the late eighteenth century that salmon began to be chilled for export from Berwick and around the town are several ice-houses, where ice was stacked in winter, and stored underground until required, to be broken up for packing around the fresh salmon when they were placed in barrels for export down the coast. Another curious export from Berwick was that of eggs and it is recorded that in 1797 more than 5,000 chests (each containing 1,600 eggs) were sent to London. At a current price of 7s. 6d. per hundred this represented an annual trade of more than £30,000, which was a substantial sum for that time.

A better known Northumbrian product is the Craster kipper and though the tiny fishing port of Craster is now almost defunct a small kippering factory still provides this local delicacy. Perhaps equally well known, as local characters, were the Cullercoats fishwives, though here at Cullercoats the fish trade has ceased completely and practically all the cottages inhabited by the fishing families have been cleared away. What were once no doubt looked upon as comfortable cottages became 'inadequate eyesores' and were demolished just before they had the opportunity to become 'quaint and desirable'.

Returning down the coast brings one again to the Tyne where, along with the Wear, one of the great industries of the North-East, that of ship-building, once developed, prospered and waned. As with so much of the region's development, one could say that ship-building flourished here as a result of the coal trade. For the export of coal, much of it down the coast to London, called for more and more ships; and following the demand for vessels came a demand for their fittings —sails, ropes, nails, chains and anchors. Hence around the Tyne and Wear a vast range of ancillary workshops, foundries and roperies sprang up in the eighteenth and nineteenth centuries. Shipyards were to be found along the river banks, and of Sunderland in the 1820s William Brockie wrote: 'The banks of the river were studded with small wood shipbuilding yards as far as the tide flowed, exciting the wonder of strangers, when they passed at time of low water, as to how the builders could possibly manage to get their vessels launched.'

It was around this time that Sunderland became widely known as a shipbuilding centre and it was then, too, that many of today's yards such as Austin, Barram, Pickersgill and Doxford began. By the middle of last century the Tyne and the Wear had become firmly established as ship-building rivers. The *John Bowes,* built by Palmers in 1852 and the first screw-propelled iron collier, was significant in this development and from then on iron ships steadily replaced wooden ones. Towns grew up where previously there had only been villages around the Palmer shipyard at Jarrow and that of Andrew Leslie at Hebburn. Armstrong's works upstream at Elswick provided another growth point and so the industry flourished.

In 1897 Charles Parsons produced *Turbinia* which revolutionised propulsion and commercial shipbuilding culminated in the launch of *Mauretania* from Swan, Hunter's yard at Wallsend in September 1906. The *Newcastle Daily Chronicle* commented: 'The anxiety to witness the launching was very great and the afternoon trains carried thousands of visitors to Wallsend, from Newcastle, Shields and elsewhere. The streets round about the yard all had a complement of townsfolk. It was indeed a gala day in the mid-river town'. For more than twenty years the *Mauretania* dominated the Atlantic. She achieved a speed of 32 knots which she maintained for 112 miles and she made 350 voyages across the Atlantic for a total of over 2,500,000 miles. Probably there is no one alive today who helped to build her, but there are still many who remember the real feeling of sadness when she returned to the river in 1935, to say farewell before going to Glasgow for breaking up. Alderman Arthur Grey, recently leader of Newcastle City Council, remembers as a child sitting upon his father's shoulders, to watch her being launched.

After the First World War north-east shipbuilding declined. A little before then, the North-East often produced in any one year two out of every five ships built in the world and indeed in the thirty years leading up to the First World War, there was only the rarest of occasions when it did not build at least a third of the world's shipping.

As the decline began, unemployment grew and a social survey, *Industrial Tyneside*, published in 1928, sadly relates the percentages of unemployed workers in the shipbuilding industry. By 1926, for example, it had risen to 61·3 per cent— 'A bitter record', as that author stated. He went on to describe the methods of employment which were then in use, fifty years ago:

'In each shipyard there are recognised places where men of the different occupations assemble; these are known as "markets", the "drillers' market", the "riveters' market", and so on. The foremen go there twice a day, at 7.30 a.m. and 1.00 p.m., to engage such men as they require. In most crafts there are "royals", i.e. men who are taken on before others when work is available. . . . In busy times the employment of many of the men may be continuous over weeks and possibly over months, but for the great majority there are frequent gaps in employment.'

To give a specific example of these fluctuations, the author quotes from one yard in 1908 which employed 960 men on one day in March, and then 1586 men on one day in June.

Let us move now from shipbuilding to the men who sailed some of these ships, for so many boys in the region have felt the urge of the sea and joined the Merchant Navy. One such was Henry Wright, born at Hartlepool in 1871, who ran away to sea and served first on sailing ships and whose diary has been preserved. He gained his 2nd Mate's certificate at the age of twenty-two and his Master's certificate when twenty-six. He got his first ship when aged thirty-two and from then on served with the shipping company of Ropners, based in Hartlepool. His voyages seem to have been surprisingly varied, as the following brief notes suggest:

		(*aboard S.S. Wandby*)
October	5th, 1906	Sailed Penarth
	13th	arrived Madeira
	25th	sailed
November	9th	arrived New York
	14th	sailed

December	2nd	Gibraltar
	8th	arrived Torre Annunciata (Italy, near Naples)
	24th	sailed
	25th	arrived Tripany (Trapani, Sicily)
January	5th, 1907	sailed
	9th	arrived Garutchie (?)
	,,	arrived Aqua Marga (?)
	12th	sailed
	14th	Gibraltar
February	7th	arrived Philadelphia
	18th	sailed
March	10th	arrived Leith
	20th	arrived Tyne

At some point around the time of the First World War Captain Wright also jotted down his crew:

Master	1
Deck Officers	2
Sailors	8
Bosun	1
Engineers	4
Firemen	9
Donkeyman	1
Apprentices	2
Cook and Stewards	4
Wireless Operator	1
	33

1 Stowaway

And now the harbour at Hartlepool is largely used for the local yachting club.

9 A Coal-Miner's Life

Many coal miners, or pitmen as they were generally called last century in the North-East, have recorded their reminiscences of underground conditions, but one of the most remarkable things which one discovers when talking to these elderly men is their lack of bitterness. Whilst listening one almost becomes more bitter on their behalf than the men themselves, who seem to have developed a special kind of gentleness through their hard experience.

One thing is quite clear, they were never given any formal training for what they would be doing underground. As Jack Kell of Leasingthorne told me: 'You were given a job to do—and if you didn't know how to do it—well, that was the time to learn! Aye! It was hard—you had to find out for yourself!'

Dick Morris of Pelton has recorded: 'There may be other jobs in life where the introduction to the way of earning a living resembles mining, but I don't know of any. If there are, the lads going to them have my deepest sympathy'. His first day down the pit remained vividly in his recollection for the rest of his life. In his own words:

'I had already been to see the manager, and he gave me a note to see the overman. This man gave me a note authorising the lamp man to give me a lamp. I went to start on the first Monday after my fourteenth birthday. We went to start at 6 a.m. prompt. As soon as I had my lamp, I was given a quick run down on how to look after it, and especially how easily it could be put out by carelessness. But, like everyone else, I had to learn this the hard way. Anyway I had my lamp, and I followed the rest of the men and lads up the steel stairway to the pitheap. I had to try hard not to show just how frightened I really was. The pit buzzer blew six o'clock; the cages were cleared, and the first lot of men stepped into the first deck of the cage, and I was amongst them. There was a rap to the engine man, and the cage was lowered to the next deck, and that was filled with men as well. There was another rap to the engineman, and we were on our way down.

For the next few seconds, I was even more frightened than ever. But I didn't get time to worry much about it before we were at the bottom, and everybody was getting smartly out of the cage to where the foreever-man was standing. He checked everyone's lamp. As I handed him my lamp, he asked me my name, "Dick Morris" I said, "Jim Morris's lad?" he asked. "Yes", I said, and he turned to another lad and told him to take me along with him and show me how to go on with the trap door.'

The pit-bottom—that area around the foot of the shaft—was brick-lined and lit by electric lights and the roof was in part brick-arched for added strength. Near here would be the stables where the pitponies were kept and the whole of this area would be roughly white-washed. It was of a comfortable height and reasonably well-lit. But away from the immediate pit-bottom the 'gate' or passage ran through the coal seam which could be seen between the stout timber props. Dick Morris had been put in the care of another lad called Tommy Mordew, who now led him along the Busty seam. This had an average thickness of five to six feet, which made it possible to walk fairly comfortably.

To be handed over as a raw newcomer to the guidance of some youth was the nearest to training that any pit lad was likely to get. Sometimes this would result in unkind jokes of a warped kind of humour, or perhaps more often in a sort of rough and ready guidance, as Dick Morris himself experienced. On this first day of his down the pit, he recollects that

'after walking for twenty minutes or so, we came to the bottom of a very steep bank, and this, I was told, led up into the Harvey seam. As we climbed, it reminded me of pictures I had seen of caves. There was little or no timber about, and the angle of ascent made it hard work climbing the steep gradient. At last we reached the bank top and Tommy Mordew told me we were in the Harvey seam. He showed me the vertical capstan wheel with which he lowered the full tubs down the bank, and at the same time this hauled the empty ones up. Then he took me a bit further in, and showed me the trapdoor that I was to open and shut to let the putter and his pony in and out. He told me to fix myself a seat, and make myself comfortable because it would be a long day.

And he was right! I thought that day would never end. The purpose of this door was to divert the fresh air coming in from the shaft into the coal face, and to make it travel around the men's working places, before being diverted back to the fan shaft. The door and its framework was quite a stout affair, and it stopped at least 95 per cent of the air from going beyond that point, but it was some yards from the main road, so the air in this small cul-de-sac was quite warm and dry. So for most of the day, I sat there in my shirt and trousers just waiting for that putter lad to come out and go back again. I think I saw him about nine or ten times during the whole of that first day.

This seam was only just being developed, and was being driven in a north easterly direction from the top of the bank. The men working in the headings were not very far away, but that first day, they might just as well have been in Timbucktoo as far as I was concerned. All I could think of was that I was alone, and very much so, for the first time in my life, and I was scared. I wandered about that small area trying to listen for the sound of Tommy, wherever he was. Now and again I could hear him and sometimes I could see him going past the entrance to my turn. But there was such a tiny light from his lamp, that it was just a ghostly shadow without shape or form. The time passed very slowly indeed. I had no watch, and I couldn't even guess the time, so every now and again I very nearly panicked. I kept on telling myself that Tommy wasn't very far away, nor the men for that matter, and I think that was what made me stay put. Tommy had told me it would be a long day, and that he would come and see me now and again. He was as good as his word and I did see him about three times all day. I found out later in the week he had a very full time job himself without bothering about me.'

What a far cry this is from the apprentice-training schemes, 'day release' and 'sandwich courses' of today's industrial training. But even if, as Dick Morris says, 'It's an experience that has lasted me a lifetime' he did at last manage to get that first shift over, and the second, and the third, and then as his confidence grew: 'I began to explore and take an interest in my new surroundings. I even got to understand Tommy's job of driving and braking the bank. He brought the tubs of coal out from the two flats, one straight on from the bank top, and one to the right hand side of this main roadway, and then he dropped them down the bank seven at a time, with the capstan wheel, and at the same time he pulled seven empty ones up.'

The amount of skilled work carried out underground, at the turn of the century may be surprising to those who have thought of the pitman as a rough man, working with his hands but not his brain; but of course a lot of this still had to be learnt the hard way by the young incomer. And no sooner had he become reasonably adept at one job then he was pushed to another. Dick Morris remembers: 'My introduction to the pit by way of being a trapper lad was short lived. I learned afterwards that this short apprenticeship was designed to act as a boost to one's morale and to get you accustomed to the atmosphere of the pit, and generally give you confidence in your new environment. So on the Monday morning, after a week at the trapdoor, the overman told me to go along with another lad and learn his job. I could scarcely believe my good fortune, because the job was driving the full tubs from the bottom of the bank where I had been the week before, out to the shaft, and taking in the empties. I knew the lad well and I couldn't understand why he should want to give up such a job, but of course he had no say in such matters, and just had to do what he was told. These shaft jobs were usually sought after and I was delighted at my good luck. It didn't take me long to learn all the details, and the next day I was going about it like an old hand. I soon found that my pony knew quite as much about the job as I did.'

Pit ponies have now almost disappeared, but at the time Dick Morris was recollecting they were commonly in use. Everybody who has worked with them tells of their 'pit sense', and a sensible lad would not only take care of his pony, but learn to observe their reactions. This is how Dick Morris remembers his time

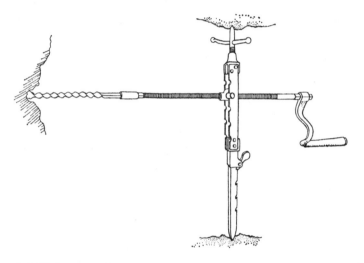

Fig. 21a.   A coal drill for use underground.
The body of the drill was jacked up between floor and roof of the mine and the light twist bit was turned to drill a hole used for shot-firing. See plate 69.

with his pony 'Clapper'. 'As soon as I got to the shaft with my load of seven full tubs', he says, 'I could unhook his limbers from the tubs whilst they were still in motion, and travelling at quite a good speed, and he would step smartly out of the way of them and they would then travel on towards the shaft under their own momentum. If I'd had to stop him to do this, I'd have had a hard job pushing them there. I could unhook his limbers in this way, and then he'd walk back to where the empty tubs were; all ready for me to hook him on again. He even knew whether I was going straight back in again, or whether I was waiting for empties.

To prove this I used to stand quite still sometimes to see if he'd move off on his own. It was my first lesson on the intelligence of pit ponies. Like everybody else

Fig. 21b.   A wooden coal shovel.
Several examples like this have been found in old northern workings, and probably date from the seventeenth or eighteenth centuries.

I soon learned to respect this peculiar instinct in them, and there were many occasions afterwards, when I was amply rewarded so far as my own safety was concerned.'

By now Dick Morris, in common with most pit lads of his age, had become resigned to his new environment. One can also, perhaps, begin to see how workers in the pit felt themselves different from surface workers. They developed a kind of 'clannishness' and even called their rough dialect speech 'pitmatic'. Naturally their experiences underground, and their very method of work in a perpetual half-light gave them this feeling of isolation.

But however much a youth may have adapted to this new underground way of working, there were times when his confidence could be severely shaken, and Dick Morris still remembers vividly what happened at the Burns Pit at West Stanley, on 16th February 1909:

'I was on my knees washing my head and body, when our next door neighbour shouted to tell us that the Burns Pit had "Gone off", (i.e. exploded underground) and as we looked out of the front room window we could see the smoke still coming from the shaft. Considering the very slow means of communication of those days, the speed with which this dreadful news spread throughout the county was nothing less than miraculous. My Dad urged me to Hurry Up. There seemed nothing for it, but to get there as quickly as possible. I remember I had a hurried bath, and I quickly swallowed my meal, and we were on our way.

'The railway line ran through our village, and it was only a matter of a couple of dozen yards from our door. The coal from most of the pits west of us was all

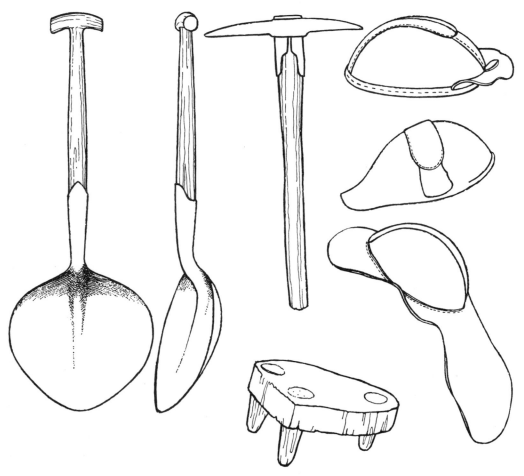

Fig. 22.   Coal mining tools and equipment of the last century.
The metal shovel has a large blade or bowl, because coal is relatively light and a large quantity could be shovelled. The pick has a short shaft, for use in a restricted working space. The cracket or working stool was used to rest the shoulder on, when working in a shallow seam. The two upper helmets are of leather and were worn by deputies, or underground foremen. See plate 65. The lower helmet, also of leather, was worn by a shaft-sinker and the long flap hung over the back of his neck, to protect him from water which would drip heavily down the shaft. See plate 75.

brought down by gravity inclines to Stella Gill, and then taken on to Tyne Dock by locomotives. We knew we could get to Stanley on these empty trucks if they were still running. The railway men told us that they were and in no time at all we were at the scene of one of the worst pit disasters in the history of the North-East. There was a vast crowd of people. Smoke was still coming from the shaft. All sorts of rumours were being passed around. No-one seemed to have any idea of the real extent of the disaster. Men were offering their services for rescue work. Only one thing seemed certain, and that was that the shaft was so badly damaged it would take some time to be put right. I can well remember the pitiful cries of the womenfolk with men in the pit, and the members of the various religious organis-ations doing their best to comfort these unfortunate people.

'As the time went by, the crowds grew bigger, until in the end I couldn't see anything at all. We'd been there now about four hours, and most people had come to accept the worst about the tragedy. Up to that point, no real hard news had been circulating about any survivors. Appeals had been made from time to time for men from the nearby pits to come forward for rescue work. Also for the crowds of people not to impede the efforts of all those who were busy with the work of getting the shafts back into working order. My impressions were of an atmosphere of gloom, and despondency. There didn't appear to be any hope of survivors.'

In fact twenty-six men and boys were saved, but 168 lives were lost. At the final count, two men were checked as missing and their bodies were only found some years later.

Tragedies of this kind have long been the lot of miners, though happily major catastrophies of this kind are now much less frequent than was the case last century. Nevertheless the immediate effect on those not involved in the disaster can be well appreciated and on such occasions the management would turn a blind eye to non-attendances for a day or two. Dick's mother was so upset that she kept him away from work next day, but on Thursday, two days after the explosion, he went back to work. 'But', he said 'I know I was as scared as ever. If I hadn't been going back to my job at the shaft bottom, I don't think I could have faced it. We did not go back to Stanley until the Sunday, the day of the funeral.'

Such funerals seem to have been watched, and recorded by the press, with a somewhat ghoulish thoroughness. Dick Morris recalls it all in vivid detail and many are the photographs, which still exist in the locality, of the coffins being borne to the mass graves. 'They were buried in two long trenches in the cemetery', he recalls, 'and I can still remember the long slow moving column of people, with a coffin every few yards, reaching back as far as the eye could see. With brass bands from every part of the county playing funeral marches. There was absolute chaos, with people fainting everywhere. Even the men carrying the coffins had to be relieved through the slowness of the processions. The situation at the churchyard was a shambles. The police force had been reinforced for the occasion, but their task was an almost impossible one. In spite of all their trying to keep people away from the churchyard itself, all the approaches to it were a mass of people. It took several hours to get all the coffins to the grave side. There was general confusion even then, over which clergyman took which burial. However well it may have been organised beforehand, all control had quickly been lost, because of the great crowds of people. I don't know how it all ended, but I'm sure that it was only because evening was coming on, and most people would have to walk home, that some order came into that dreadful scene. I heard afterwards that the massive grave was filled in the next day. There were local services throughout the county, and a fund was started to help the stricken families.'

Such funds were all too common an occurrence. Sometimes small souvenirs were printed, or cheap wine glasses or glass water jugs would be engraved with the date and the number of lives lost. These were then sold to raise money for the bereaved families.

But after all this, work still had to continue and would be back to normal quite soon. 'I really came to enjoy those few weeks at the shaft bottom', says Dick Morris, 'but all too suddenly it became my turn to teach a new lad the job, and I was sent off to a far more remote part of the pit. On the first morning I went to start on this new job, there were about a dozen of us in the group going to different parts of that district. We were gathered at our first dispersal point waiting to have our lamps examined by the deputy. The conversation was the usual lively one for a Monday morning. My mind was occupied with my new job, and my first contact, on my own, with the pit, a long way from the shaft. Suddenly, there was a very loud explosion, which shook the whole place violently. My thoughts went immediately to the Stanley pit explosion, and I was terrified. But one of the older lads said "It's all right Dicky, it's only the sinkers firing a shot at the new stapple."'

A 'stapple' is a fairly shallow shaft joining the workings in two seams and what the pit-boy had heard was work going on in another part of the pit, where a new seam, called the Townley Seam, was being opened up, and the coal from those new workings was to be lowered to the Busty seam and then drawn to the surface by the main shaft. Complexities of this kind soon become the everyday experience of the pitman and helped to heighten that isolation from the above-ground community already mentioned.

The working knowledge of the youth was now being extended: 'This time I was collecting the tubs two or three at a time from the flat, and driving them to the rope-end, where another lad was hanging them on to the endless ropeway which was then carrying them on to the shaft. At the shaft, I'd been working partly under electric lights, and partly with my safety lamp. Now I was completely dependent on my safety lamp, and I was beginning to realise the vast difference. At the shaft, you had height, light and plenty of air. Now, for the first time in my life, I began to understand what pit work was all about—I couldn't stand upright, but had to spend the whole day slightly stooped, with my head coming into violent contact with the roof every now and again. But I soon learned to keep down!

The air was very warm and dry, and away from the main ropeway, what we call in pit talk, very slack, meaning there wasn't much of it. As for my lamp, at first I had quite a job to see anything at all, but after a while I was very surprised how quickly I got used to it.'

These tubs, used to carry the coal from the coal-face to the shaft, were small, built originally of wood, but later of steel. They ran on four small flanged wheels

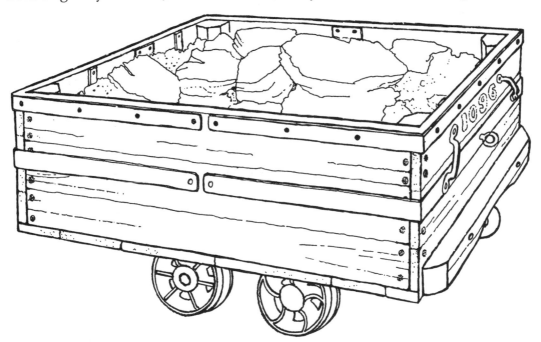

Fig. 23.   Underground coal 'tub'.
Contrast this with a lead-ore tub. (Fig. 8). The coal tub was used in a shallow seam, hence it is fairly large in plan, but not very high.

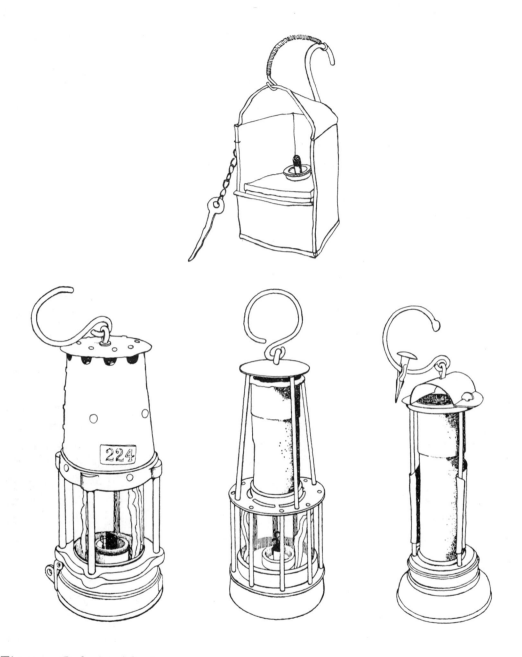

Fig. 24. Coal miners' lamps.
Above is a midgy *lamp with a naked flame used in a 'safe' pit, i.e. one without gas. Such lamps were in use into the early years of this century. The other three lamps are safety lamps, where the flame is protected by a fine wire gauze. That on the right is the earliest, perhaps about 1830 or 1840. The nail was driven into a pit prop, to support the lamp while the miner worked at the coal face.*

and were fairly squat because of the thinner seams where they were used (Fig. 23). It is interesting to contrast them with the quite different tubs used in lead mines (Fig. 8 and Plate 21). The lead tub could be higher, but was much narrower because of the narrow vertical vein from which the ore was taken.

To return to the coal mine, the tubs were brought from the hewer, who worked at the coal face, by the putter. He would be a young man, hoping soon to be a hewer. Dick Morris thinks the putter lads had the hardest job in the pit: 'There were usually several hewers in each district, and it was the putter's job to see that each man was kept supplied with empty tubs. To give him an added incentive, the deputy would see that he had a place where he could go and hew some coal for himself whenever he had any spare time. And although their job was a hard one, this added incentive generally became almost an obsession, and very few of them could resist the urge to take full advantage of this peculiar system. It really was hard work, and my most vivid memories are of a lad in the shortest of shorts, (pit hoggers as we called them) the scantiest of shirts, sweating and slushing (a typical Durham expression for being in a hell of a hurry) back and forth between the men, and his own place; cussing his head off, and often walloping his pony unmercifully in an attempt to get a few more bob a week, or rather fortnight as we were then paid. The sole ambition of most of these lads was to go on and become a fully fledged coal hewer.'

The progression was from trapper to driver, driver to putter and putter to coal hewer. The average putter/coal hewer phase probably lasted from about the age of twenty to around fifty with slight variations. By the age of about fifty a man's stamina would begin to decline and he would soon be looking for a 'datal job'. These men did most of the repair work anywhere in the pit. If a man's lungs got badly affected by silicosis he might be lucky enough to get a job 'at bank on the screens'. That is to say, he would end his working life helping to sort out the lumps of shale from the coal as it moved past on a mechanically-powered belt (See plate 74).

Without, one hopes, appearing too morbid, it is probably appropriate to end this section on the typical life of a north-eastern pit worker, by referring to two underground accidents which Dick Morris recalled from his early days down the pit. Both turned out to be fatal, though possibly neither need have been and the very words of his recollections emphasise the changes which have taken place in working conditions over sixty years:

'I hadn't been at the shaft bottom many days before I saw something that has left its mark to this day. I had already seen one or two non-fatal accident cases, and seen the difficulty of getting the injured men from the shaft bottom to the surface. It left a great deal to be desired. The cages were not wide enough to take a stretcher at full length, so the stretchers were hinged in the middle. It's amazing to look back on it, but they really were hinged.

'When this poor fellow was brought to the shaft bottom, he was obviously in a serious condition. He'd survived a very rough passage from the place where he'd been injured. He had been badly crushed about the middle part of his body, but to me he seemed to be fairly comfortable. But when the cages were cleared, and the stretcher had to be got ready to be put into the cage, he began to protest. It was so obvious that any movement involving the middle part of his body was going to be terribly painful. All those around him tried to explain that it was absolutely necessary to bend the stretcher to get it into the cage, and that this was necessary in order to get him to hospital. Though how this was to be done I hadn't the faintest idea. The more the men tried to bend the stretcher, however carefully, the more distressed he became, until he was almost screaming with pain, and begging them to leave him alone.

'By now I was in tears, and one of the men took me away from that horrible scene. I know they did eventually get him to the surface, but he was dead by the time they got him home. At that time the only way they could have got him to the hospital would have been by coal cart. And the hospital was in Newcastle, seven miles away, so I doubt whether he'd have lived through that journey. The second accident was very similar, except that the man was unconscious when he reached the shaft bottom. He came round for a short while, as they got the stretcher ready to put him into the cage. He groaned in his agony and begged them to leave him alone. He also died before they got him home.'

One can hardly wonder, after such experiences, that the pitmen of the North-East have not only hated the coal-owners, but the pits themselves. Though a curious kind of love-hate relationship has often bound the men to their work and such a tough life drew together the whole population of each pit village. This community spirit, which in the nineteenth century had stood firm despite evictions and 'blacklegs', held through the first half of the present century. It was a spirit the equal of which would be difficult to find in any other industry. But it has now largely gone, weakened by pit closures, by new housing, by improved working conditions, by education, by greater spending power and by the mass media. One may regret its loss, but welcome most of the means whereby it was destroyed.

10 The Pitman's Cottage

'The old-time houses are a standing witness of the opinion those who built them had of the workmen'
(John Wilson in *History of the Durham Miners' Association* 1870–1904, published 1907.)

This statement, while in large part justified, was perhaps too strong an indictment, for many pit houses were at least as good if not better than the country cottages out of which workers moved when emigrating to the nineteenth-century coalfield.

Yet the strangest stories were believed about northern pitmen and some nineteenth-century writers doubted that miners lived in houses at all. William Cobbett, describing the coal districts through which he passed during his Northern Tour in 1832, wrote: 'Here is the most surprising thing in the world; thousands of men and thousands of horses continually living underground; children born there, and who sometimes, it is said, seldom see the surface at all, though they live to a considerable age.' Cobbett was probably gullible enough to have been misled by an early Geordie humourist!

Cobbett, however, was not alone in his ignorance, for stories abound of visitors of less radical mind than he, who held this belief. The following example is taken from Boyle's volume on Durham County: 'Some years ago a gentleman came into the North to fill an important position in a large colliery. He arrived late at night and slept at the Inn. The following morning, on looking out, he immediately called the landlord, and asked what all those cottages were for. 'Cottages, Sir? Those are the pitmen's houses.' 'Good gracious!' exclaimed the southerner, 'I thought pitmen lived in the pit!'

The first detailed descriptions of miners' living conditions are contained in the 1841 report of the Commission on Child Employment, and particularly the descriptions written on Durham by J. R. Leifchild (later used by him in the Travellers' Library series: *Our Coal and Our Coal-Pits,* 1853). Leifchild described three categories of houses he had seen in Durham: two-roomed houses, where both rooms were on the ground floor, and two-roomed houses, which were 'one up and one down', and three-roomed houses which had two ground floor rooms and one upper floor room.

The earliest plan of a northern miner's dwelling may well be one drawn up for the Stella Company in 1838. This shows a simple dwelling with one upper room and one lower room, with a small pantry attached at the rear. It was probably one of the commonest kind of pit house in Northumberland and Durham last century. Its rather cramped upper floor seems to have been typical of this design and was approached by a steep ladder.

Of about the same period was a group of houses standing until recently at Gurney Valley near Bishop Auckland. They were probably built by Backhouses soon after the sinking of the Black Boy Colliery in 1830, and are of the kind described by Angus Watson in *My Life* as 'two living-rooms that were a kitchen and a bedroom, with a garret overhead where the children slept.' This was certainly quite a common design which may have been related to earlier rural dwellings, and it continued to be built up to around 1870.

Increased prosperity in the late 1860s and early 1870s, combined with increased pressure from the miners for better housing conditions, eventually produced the substantial four-roomed dwelling.

Very little of the pre-1870 housing now remains and what there is has generally been much altered, so we must turn to written descriptions. Fortunately, between 1873 and 1874, the *Newcastle Weekly Chronicle* published a series of articles entitled 'Our Colliery Villages', which referred to mining villages in both Durham and Northumberland commenting upon the provision of facilities for recreation, learning and worship as well as housing and sanitary conditions.

The houses were generally constructed of rubble stone and slated, though brick and even timber houses were constructed, the latter particularly where they were intended only to be short-lived (though like the more recent 'pre-fabs' of the late 1940s they often outlived their planned life-span). Pantiles were often used for roofing until the 1840s and 50s, when Welsh blue slates became readily available with the coming of the railways. Many houses, it also has to be noted, were originally pantiled but have been subsequently re-roofed with slates.

The floor of earlier cottages would be beaten earth (as Leifchild observed at Coxhoe in 1841) and later they would have stone-flagged floors, but most probably had 'bricks laid flat', or 'quarrels'—thick, red square tiles. Later wooden floors were laid in the downstairs front rooms and from the 1870s onwards concrete was increasingly used for kitchen floors.

The upper floors were often built without ceilings, although ceiling the attics

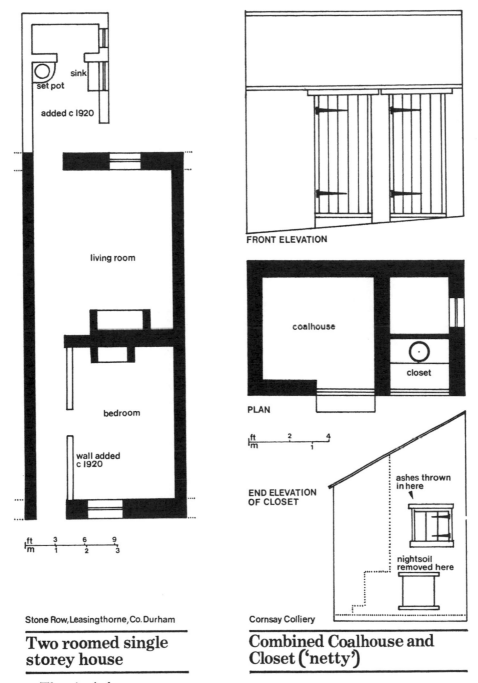

sink

set pot

added c 1920

living room

bedroom

wall added c 1920

ft   3   6   9
m   1   2   3

Stone Row, Leasingthorne, Co. Durham

Two roomed single storey house

FRONT ELEVATION

coalhouse

closet

PLAN

ft   2   4
m   1

END ELEVATION OF CLOSET

ashes thrown in here

nightsoil removed here

Cornsay Colliery

Combined Coalhouse and Closet ('netty')

Fig. 25. The miner's house.
Left *a typical plan of one single-storey cottage in a terrace.*
Right *details, to a larger scale, of a little out-house which typically served pit cottages.*

was one of the first improvements carried out from the 1850s onwards. In the downstairs rooms the joists supporting the floor of the upper room were usually left bare by the builders, but occupants often pasted brown paper beneath to provide a 'ceiling' and sometimes covered this with cheap deorative wallpaper. According to a report of the Medical Officer of Health, who inspected houses at Ryhope in 1937, nearly every house had at least one room with papered joists and a native of Ferryhill Station remembered that this was a common practice by the early years of this century.

The floorboards of the upper storey were sometimes laid loose upon the joists and George Parkinson describing an early prayer-meeting in a pitman's cottage mentions this and says that 'the host, sure that the house would be full, took up every third board in the loft, so that those upstairs could hear though they could not see'. Perhaps also, loose boards would facilitate the movement of large pieces of bedroom furniture into the upper room. In 'one up and one down' cottages at Bedlington, now demolished, the bedroom floor was fixed but had a large trap door to serve this purpose, for the steep ladder provided as staircase came through a much smaller aperture.

In the first half of last century if a miner's house had an upper floor it was invariably reached by a ladder, often set almost vertically. Dr J. Wilson wrote of the Long Row at Haswell: 'the houses were of the back to back kind. There were two rooms: the kitchen and the room upstairs, with a straight-up ladder as the mode of reaching it.' The upper floor would be entered through a small trapdoor, or just an opening in the bedroom floor. Albert Flatman, aged eighty-two in 1974, a retired colliery blacksmith and a native of Mainsforth, recalled that he used to sleepwalk as a child so his mother had to be especially careful about shutting their trapdoor. This could be an even more perilous affliction for those living in cottages where the colliery company had dispensed with even a trapdoor. Sometimes there was not even a handrail round this opening in the bedroom floor.

Gradually through the second half of last century the ladders became less steep, and the steps were eventually boxed to provide more conventional staircases. It is interesting to learn from the records of the Stella Coal Company that as early as 1860 Joseph Hedley suggested that staircases should be fitted in their new houses and his idea was accepted, though many families had to put up with ladders until well into this century.

Certain items of furniture might be built into the miner's cottage and Ernst Duckershoff, a German miner working at Walbottle in Northumberland in the 1890s, wrote 'dwellings are so constructed here that there is not space for a great quantity of furniture and the principal items are built into the rooms'. William

Kelly (aged eighty-seven in 1975), a retired miner from Ferryhill added further detail. He recalled his father mentioning that if a man entered into a bond with a colliery company and obtained a house, but did not have his own furniture, the colliery joiners would construct for him a simple four-poster bed. Similarly cupboards were commonly built into cottages, and occasionally there would be a built-in 'settle' near the fire. This was simply a stout plank let into the wall at each end, with the wall as support for the back.

In the kitchen-living room, a large metal range containing a baking oven, a boiler for heating water, and a fire grate, was probably commonly fitted by colliery companies by the late 1850s and a number survive to this day, though by now quite uncommon. There were several variations, particularly in the shape of the ovens, for these were often round with circular doors; it has been suggested that these were earlier than square ovens. Some boilers were provided with a tap, for ease in drawing off the hot water, but earlier ones were merely open at the top, with a hinged metal lid and water was collected by dipping in a 'lading can'. Sometimes the colliery company would also provide a set pot in the scullery for clothes washing.

As to the windows of these houses, these have undergone so many changes that it is difficult to decide what was their earliest form. Probably they tended to be about 5 feet 6 inches high and 3 feet 6 inches wide, with vertically sliding sashes, with sixteen or eighteen small panes, though horizontally sliding sashes of smaller dimensions have been recorded in the Hetton area. Surprising as it may be to modern eyes, most miners' dwellings seem to have had wooden shutters to the windows on the ground floor, fastened against the house wall during the day and closed at night, after the lamp was lit in the kitchen. An elderly man at Causey remembered that, in his village the shutters were painted on one side only—that which could be seen in daylight! He further recalled that by about 1920 only older people continued to use shutters, though some were brought back into use by the 'blackout' of the second world war. After that brief revival they seem to have completely disappeared.

Many pitmen's houses had half-doors, of the kind more commonly associated with stables, though a terrace at Causey combined these with the more conventional door, so that the occupant could either close out the weather completely, or utilise the half door on a warm evening, for a 'bit crack' with a neighbour. Half doors, elderly women recollect, were also very useful on a hot baking day for they provided welcome ventilation without cold draughts.

Most houses, whatever their design, had a small pantry or scullery, generally projecting from the main building and often about six feet square. It would either be floored with the same materials as the kitchen-living room or in some inferior material. Thus, for example, the specifications for the Stella Coal Company provided bricks for the pantry, but stone flags for the kitchen. Normally it would be provided with shelves and a small window.

By the 1860s water supplies began to be available provided by the newly established Water Companies; gas lighting also began to appear and improvements in public health legislation gradually changed living conditions. Thus communal water taps were placed along the back streets, not unlike fire-hydrant stand pipes and 'slop stones' would be placed in the sculleries to serve as primitive sinks. Earth closets were generally constructed, one to every two houses, across the yard or street, associated with the ashpit where ash from the fire was tipped. These were frequently devised in such way that the ash would mix with the excreta at ground level provided that the lid was in position in the vacant 'netty' when the ash was tipped. (See Fig. 25) Though there is at least one recollection of a housewife bitterly at odds with her neighbour, who waited until the poor woman went to the 'netty' and then proceeded to tip a bucketful of ash down the adjoining ash pit.

Ovens of various shapes have been mentioned, often having been provided as part of the kitchen range, but communal brick bread ovens standing in the open air seem to have been commonly constructed in the first half of last century. These, possibly to be seen as descendants of the mediaeval oven or bakehouse, were to be found in areas where the houses were not provided with adequate individual ovens. None seem to have survived in the north, though plate 97 was taken early this century somewhere along the Tyne near Prudhoe, and 1856 ordnance survey maps show outbuildings which are almost certainly bread ovens. But most of these had disappeared by the time of the 1896 edition of these maps.

These ovens did not have a chimney. Each simply comprised a circular space with domed roof, perhaps three feet across, which was heated by a fire subsequently raked out. Sometimes (as in plate 97) a space was provided below to take these embers. The oven would be closed by a metal door, also visible in the plate. They were generally situated at the end or in the centre of a row of houses, though sometimes they were placed next to, or even as part of, a block of 'conveniences', as in houses at Ryton built by the Stella Company. Here the small block of outbuildings provided the following (reading from one end to the other): oven, privvy, ash midden, privvy, oven.

Dick Morris, born at Pelton Fell in 1895, recalls a conversation with an older man about housing conditions 'when the shafts were first sunk'. At this time one communal oven had been provided for each street and they were used 'for twenty years until each house was provided with its own baking facilities'. In one of the

Newcastle Weekly Chronicle articles on 'Our Colliery Villages', there is mention of a visit to Harton (which had been built about 1830–40), where 'ovens, ash-holes and coal places are thrown into unpleasant prominence'.

Such ovens were used in a simple, relatively primitive way, almost exactly the same as that employed 1600 years earlier by Roman soldiers on Hadrian's Wall. J. C. Reed in *A History of Ryton* gives a good description: 'When few cottages had an oven, there was what was called a brick oven in most districts. Each woman took it in turn to prepare the oven. She would collect firewood beforehand. Early on the morning of baking-day the inside of the oven was cleaned out, the wood put inside, lighted and kept burning until the right heat had been reached. The embers were then removed, the oven floor wiped clean with a cloth, and it was ready for the first bake of loaves, enough to last the household a week.'

An article in the Hexham Courant and describing Ryton in about 1840 refers to 'six to eight round loaves being cooked at a time' and adds that the baking time was one hour. 'When these were cooked, another neighbour brought her loaves to bake and so on until all had used it.'

Finally mention should be made of two other buildings often to be found not far from the pit houses—the pigeon 'cree' and the pigstye. Unlike the latter, the former was not for food production, but for the pitmen's leisure hours and these still persist though now more commonly in 'allotments' away from the houses.

The pig stye has now disappeared from the pitmens' scene, banished by byelaws, but during much of last century the pig provided a much-needed addition to the miner's diet and the styes were kept close at hand. The *Colliery Guardian* in 1863 carried a report of the opening of the Pease Company's 'model village' at Waterhouses, where each house had been provided with a pig-stye, and one of 'Our Colliery Villages' articles in 1873, describing Barrington Street, Hetton le Hole, states 'the house looks out upon a very long and neat garden, at the end of which is a piggery and privvy'. A plan exists of 'conveniences' at the rear of houses at Tudhoe Colliery, in County Durham (of about 1875) and each block provided (reading from end to end): ash pit, privvy, coalhouse, pig stye, pig stye, coalhouse, privvy, ash pit.

Mr Morris of Pelton Fell recollects that 'nearly everybody had a pig' and Mr William Kelly of Mainsforth remembers two pigs being kept, 'one for pork and one for bacon'. But swine fever, first recognised in this country in 1862 and made notifiable in 1879, seems to have discouraged pig keeping on this scale. Mr Morris recalls the first notifiable outbreak at Pelton Fell in about 1900 and the mass slaughter of the pigs and their carcasses being burned in the colliery gashouse fires. Few people continued to keep pigs afterwards. And the Bye-Laws of the early twentieth century discouraged them further. Section 12 of the 1902 Bye-Laws of Bishop Auckland, for example, stated 'The occupier of any premises shall not keep any swine or deposit any swine's dung, within the distance of ninety feet from any dwelling house. . . .'

11 Life in a Pit Village

The text of this chapter is largely based upon recollections of Mr George Bell of Bishop Auckland, a retired miner who was born in 1884 and who gave his recollections to the North of England Open Air Museum in 1968, when he was aged eighty-four.

FURNITURE

Most miners' homes had a picture of Queen Victoria hanging in a prominent place in the kitchen. This was the room where the family spent most of their waking hours, when in the house. A picture of William Gladstone was also a strong favourite since many miners held liberal opinions. Another was 'Geordie and the Bairn', a picture of a miner nursing his child after arriving home from the pit and before being washed and changed. It seems remarkable that something so near to real life as this should have been so popular, but so it was. Enlarged family photographs were also often to be found, well-framed and hung on the walls of many of the rooms. Pictures of all kinds were a favourite decoration and the mantelpiece was the place for all kinds of odds and ends.

Rocking chairs were fashionable and almost all homes would have at least one, and sometimes two. There were also small rocking chairs intended for use by the children, for sitting still was not much in favour even then!

A 'longsettle' was often to be found in the kitchen. This was about six or seven feet long and some eighteen inches to two feet deep, made of common deal with a fixed back. It could be moved about the room, and on cold nights could be pulled up in front of the fire. It would be capable of seating five or six persons and often used when having company for the night. Most miner's wives had 'antimacassas', which were used for covering chair backs and sofas. These were mostly home-knitted and beautiful designs could be created. In particular these would be used for the 'sitting room' suite and they were fondly believed to improve the appearance of the room and furniture. Sometimes they would be found on kitchen furniture as well, especially when there was no 'best room'.

Nearly all miner's homes, and especially those where there was a family, had a chiffonier bed. This was a folding bedstead which, when not in use, folded up to look like an ordinary chest or cupboard with two swing doors in front (Fig. 26). It was often used in the kitchen, which was always warm since the fire was kept alive all night. Chiffoniers or, as they were sometimes called, dess-beds, were mostly used by the children of the family and very snug they could be too! The top was often used for ornaments of various designs, since the chiffonier was made to look rather like a sideboard.

Fireside fittings were an outstanding feature in many miners' homes, made of steel or brass and the fender top would also be made in many and varied designs. All these items were kept highly polished and beside the fender was the 'tidy betty', a metal item which kept the ashes from spreading out onto the hearth. Sometimes this was made of shaped steel, part black and part shiny. Sometimes

Fig. 26.   A dess bed.
When the doors were opened a bed could be unfolded. During the day time this bed looked like a sideboard.

it would be decoratively made of cast iron. The hob was a loose decorated bar which fitted on top of the fire grate and was used to rest kettles and pans on, when items were being kept warm. Also on the hearth would be the coal rake, a large poker and a blazier or 'sooker'. This was a sheet of metal with a handle on it which could be held in front of the fire to make it draw, when it was not burning very well. Friday was the day when all these metal items were cleaned and polished, ready for putting down on Saturday noon for the weekend.

The fireplaces were large and mostly constructed of metal, with a set pot at one side of the fire for boiling the water and on the other side a large oven. Sometimes these ovens were round, with circular doors; sometimes they were square. It was often said that the circular ones were the best for baking bread, but of course this was often believed in the areas where circular ovens were most common.

The polishing of these fireplaces was a weekly task, using black lead. It was a job which meant a lot of hard work to obtain a good polish and in the course of this a lot of black-lead often got onto the cleaner and her clothing.

The fireplaces had large firebacks and a bucket of coal would be thrown up onto this and raked forward onto the fire as required. Of course one has to remember that coal was cheap, indeed it was given to the miners as part of their emoluments. A good fire-back would hold at least two bucketfuls of coal and generally lasted all day and night.

As most cottages had stone floors in the kitchen and scullery (if there was one) hearthrugs or mats were necessary and helped to give some feeling of warmth in the room where the family spent most of their time. Sometimes oil cloth was used as a cover over the flagstones, and this certainly improved their appearance. Even the front room, which might have a wooden floor, would be covered in oil-cloth as also were the bedrooms. Carpets were very rare at the turn of the century and apart from oilcloth only mats would be found on the floor. These mats would be clippy mats or proggy mats, made by pushing short lengths of clipped pieces of old clothing through a piece of hessian or sacking. The process of 'progging' or pushing these pieces through the hessian was carried out with a 'progger' or short pointed tool sometimes made of wood and sometimes of metal. One of the most nostalgic items of these homes was the progger, which any housewife of today can usually recognise as having been used by her mother or grandmother. The very mats themselves had a kind of 'social scale' down which they passed, for the newest one would be used in front of the hearth. When it became more worn it would be moved under the table or to the back of the room and would finally finish up as a doormat, near the door.

celluloid

cardboard

wood

metal

paper

Fig. 27. *Quilting templates.*
Templates of wood, metal, cardboard, celluloid etc. were used to mark out the elaborate patterns which were then stitched to hold wadding between two cotton or satteen sheets. See plate 115.

There would be no curtains on the windows, but instead blinds would be fitted on rollers, one fixed at the top of each window and pulled up or down by a cord at the side. These were very effective and could be bought in many colours and designs and used simply as decoration, as well as preventing anyone looking in. People thought as much about the smart appearance of their blinds as any other part of the home.

As to light in the house, there would be paraffin lamps of various sizes and designs and wax and tallow candles. The living room or kitchen, in which the family lived, would be lit by a paraffin lamp. Sometimes this stood on the table, and in other houses it would hang from the ceiling, or from a bracket fixed to the wall in a suitable place. Candles were used when moving about from one room to another or when going to bed, and many designs of candlesticks could be found. They had wide rims which caught the dripping grease spilling from the candle as it was being carried. Wax candles were used whenever available, since the tallow candle spilled more easily and gave a poorer light. Moreover they were easily melted and only used because they were cheaper.

Finally one should mention the use of screens in a miner's home. Most such houses had at least one screen and some had two or more. These were about six feet high and in panels of two feet wide. The smallest ones had two panels and others had anything from three to four panels which could be folded up when not in use. Most of them were papered over, in various designs, often decorated with 'scraps' which were small coloured pictures which could be bought in packets for a few coppers, cut out and stuck on. Screens were used in cases of illness, to prevent draughts around the patient's bed. They were also used during cold winter nights to prevent draughts from bad fitting doors and windows, thus helping to keep the room warm and cosy. Where there were large families of boys and girls the screen also came in useful to separate them when there was only one bedroom, and again the screen came into its own on bath night in isolating the person who was being bathed in front of the fire.

The miner and his family had to bath in the kitchen, and a large sized zinc or tin bath was used for this purpose. It was filled with hot water from the set pot and when the miner bathed, on return from work, he generally wore a pair of short trunks, but often did not wash his back. There was a belief that if he did so it would cause a backache and loss of work. Mr Bell remembers having seen many miners with their backs unwashed when they were changing their clothing for sports and other games, even as late as 1916.

The tin bath would hang on a hook outside the back door of the cottage when not in use and the water would be drawn from a tap in the yard or back street.

CLOTHING

The miner's wife and daughters generally took great pride in their dress and figures, until middle-aged spread prevailed. They wore steel-braced corsets to this end and twenty inch waists were quite common and looked very smart when they were really 'dressed up'. Some of their skirts were so long that they had to be held by hand or by a small metal attachment hanging from the belt, thus preventing the skirt from trailing in the mud and dust.

Ladies' dress then always included a hat, when going out for a visit. Scarves and squares on the head were not worn as they have been in more recent years, nor were bare heads. Generally flannel, cotton or woollen material was worn, as these were considered to be the best for warmth next to the skin. Mr Bell states that he cannot remember shoes being worn then, but only boots were worn even by the ladies. Sometimes these were laced and others would be buttoned up the front or the side; some were elastic sided and just pulled on. The men sometimes wore buttoned boots as well and button hooks were a necessity, to be carried wherever one went in case they were required when changing, or if a button became loose when one was away from home. These buttons could not readily be fastened up by hand.

Most people had work boots and the lighter boots which were worn with their best clothing. Men wore hobnailed boots with toe plates and heel plates of iron, since the roads and footpaths in winter were generally covered with mud. To keep their footwear waterproof dubbin or some other sort of grease or oil was used, and in bad weather the boots would be put upon the hearth to dry out for the next day. In large families it was quite hard work scraping and cleaning the dried mud from the boots before they were used again and some families were trained to clean their own, but in most cases it was the mother's job. She was often up at five o'clock in the morning or earlier and would cook breakfast for the workers in the house before they left for the pit. Brown boots were seldom seen as the mud ruined them if one was caught out in a storm or rain. Getting a shine on the boots at that time required some 'elbow grease' with nothing more than ordinary blacking to be used on them. Mr Bell recollects that socks were not worn then, only stockings and these had probably been knitted at home. Nearly every good housewife that he saw was busy knitting even when having a gossip, and of course they would knit the thick blue worsted stockings as well as black stockings to be worn with best clothes.

The better type of miner sometimes wore spats when he was dressed up and he looked very smart, though liable to a lot of friendly banter and backchat from some of the other miners who were not of the dressy type. Spats were of course used by the parson, schoolmaster and colliery officials—hence the banter. Good boots were about 12s. 6d. a pair and would be made of leather.

Straw hats or 'bengies' as they were called were used as headgear in summer and when dressed for 'going out'. Young men in particular, when out walking for pleasure always carried a walking stick. These would be home-made ones or bought ones with all kinds of designs of handles, mostly silver-headed. Such a walking stick was a social symbol, as also were ash and malacca canes. Umbrellas were quite common but mostly used by the womenfolk, for the working man who used one was usually looked upon as 'soft' by the majority.

In winter and cold weather woollen home-knitted cuffs were worn by men women and children. These were slipped over the hand and covered the wrist and part of the back of the hand and it was said that if you kept the wrist and ankles warm the rest of the body would also be warm. Mitts were also worn in winter weather, with a shaped thumb and the rest of the fingers altogether in the other part and not separated as in a glove. Knitted gloves would also be commonly used, though kid gloves were only worn by a few miners. They were supposed to be the prerogative of professionals, businessmen and colliery officials.

Blacksmiths wore fustian trousers as also did some miners, since it was a tough wearing material, warm to wear and capable of withstanding sparks. Miners and hewers sometimes used them to travel to work though when on the coal face they took them off and worked in a pair of shorts or 'hoggers'.

Long trousers were worn with a lining and required no separate underwear or lose linings as today. In Mr Bell's recollection unlined trousers and turn-ups came in in the early years of this century and gradually became common to wear as now. Some miners wives made the linings of flannelette which fastened at the knees with tape bands, until the time when underwear was taken over by business firms specialising in this type of clothing.

Many people wore red flannel belts and vests about six or seven inches wide, and one round the lower part of the back fastened by two tapes at the front. These were supposed to prevent them taking cold on their kidneys and the vest was also an assistance in preventing taking a chill.

The hardest part of the life of a miner's wife was wash day, especially when she had a family. To start with the water had to be boiled on the fire before being used in the tub. Some poss tubs were made locally by the joiner, but a great many consisted of old paraffin oil barrels cut down to size. The poss stick was a three pronged staff, or a solid block of wood shaped out to 'knead' the clothes when beaten down upon them by the force of the woman using it.

The mangle was a huge metal-framed affair worked by a system of cog wheels fixed to a driving wheel which was turned by hand. The rollers were of a particularly hard kind of wood and this again necessitated a lot of energy. The washtub fitted underneath the draining board of the mangle and when not in use the mangle and tub were usually kept in the yard if there was one, or in the scullery if possible, where it would be out of sight.

The drying of the clothes would be done in any open space near at hand, or in the back yard if the house had one. In most cases it was easier and better to dry them indoors and to do this a clothes horse would be used near the fire, covered in wet clothes. These were fairly large and had four or five rails on each side. A large hot fire soon dried a day's washing.

Ironing the clothes meant a great deal of hard work for there were no ironing boards or electric irons then. The clothes were usually ironed-out on the kitchen table with a suitable covering for the job and flat irons were used which were heated on the fire before being wiped on a soaped brown paper sheet. Two or three irons were used at a time, no time thus being wasted by waiting for them to heat.

FOOD

It will be clear from the foregoing that most miner's wives were very hard working, washing and cleaning and cooking for their family. Pot-pies were very popular as were rabbit pies made with fresh wild rabbits which cost a shilling a couple. Ham and egg pies, girdle cakes and oven cakes were all good substantial food, as were various kinds of boiled puddings such as spotted dick, suet dumplings and treacle dumplings. Large teacakes were often made with plenty of currants in them, not one or two as now! And fresh herring could be bought at twenty for a penny from fish hawkers every week in the season. There were of course no electric ovens then and the coal-fired oven, whether round or square, had to cook everything.

Milk was a penny a pint and could be got from the nearest farm. It was a job which the children had to do before going to school in the morning and sometimes the evening as well. Old milk could be bought for a penny a quart and many housewives used this when baking bread. Naturally no-one bought bread in those days. Flour was bought by the stone and kept in a large bin in the pantry, where the house had one, or otherwise in any convenient cool corner.

Mr Bell recollects that coffee was more used then for breakfast than it is now—not ready ground coffee, but coffee beans which were ground before each meal. He recollects that the majority of houses had a hand coffee grinder, which provided another job for the bairns.

As most of the miners on the western fringe of the Durham coalfield had left

94.   *A Rookhope fireside about 1900. The round oven seems to have been a peculiarity of this coalfield. Not only was the door circular, but the oven was cylindrical.*

95.   *Frank Hands, a retired pitman, at his fireside at Shiremoor in Northumberland in 1962.*

97.   *An outdoor bread oven near Ryton in the Tyne valley, around 1900. Not one of these is now known to survive and this is possibly a unique photograph of what was once a fairly common pit village feature.*

96.   *Bella Davidson by her fireside, with a visitor at Shiremoor in 1965. The brass 'line' or rail over the fire was used to air clothes.*

98.   *A Durham Leek Club group in the 1930s.*

99.   *A pigeon cree, possibly near Stanley around 1900. This is a fairly simple example, but many were elaborately decorated and painted. It was thought that this would help the pigeons to identify their home from afar.*

100.   *This photograph speaks for itself!*

101. *A group of men at South Shields in 1926, squatting 'on their hunkers'—a familiar position often adopted by miners.*

LIFE IN OTHER INDUSTRIES

102. *Quarrying limestone at Marsden in East Durham, 1892.*

103. *The old glass bottle works at Seaham Harbour.*

104. *Jack Hunter and Brian Kyle (striker) making their last chain at Winlaton, Durham, in 1966 when the last hand-making chain works in the North-East closed.*

105. *Weaving flat wire rope at Sunderland, in about 1908, at Messrs Glaholm and Robson. This firm started in 1859 and closed in 1968. This was a difficult process, requiring special hammers to separate the heavy warp wires, between which the warp wire was then drawn.*

106. *A group of chainsmiths outside Bagnall's workshop at Winlaton, about 1900. Chain-making was an industry brought to the North-East in the seventeenth-century and it prospered at Swalwell until the end of the Napoleonic Wars. Subsequently it kept going, on a smaller scale in and around the village of Winlaton.*

107. *A team of six strikers, in the South Shields area. Such a team worked to a careful rhythm in order to strike systematically on to the white-hot forging. Forgings would include very heavy constructions such as the rudder frame for a large ship.*

108. *Making shell cases at a munition works at Birtley, County Durham in 1916.*

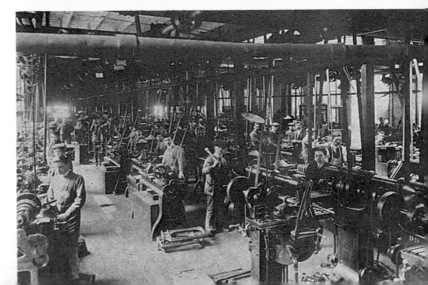

109. *An engineering works early this century: that of Reyrolles at Hebburn on the Tyne.*

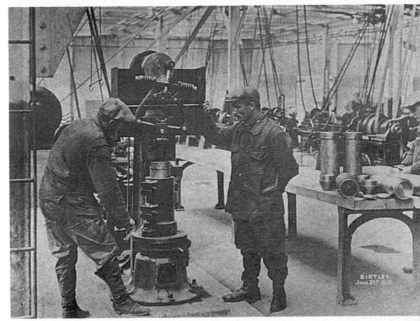

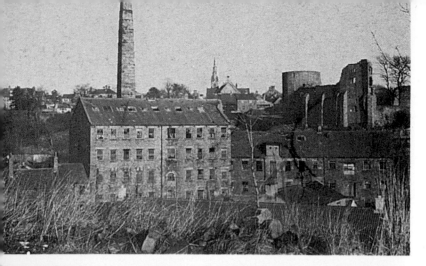

110. *Ullathorne's Mill at Startforth, just across the River Tees from Barnard Castle, was built in the early nineteenth-century and produced linen thread. It was demolished in 1975.*

111. *Cutting small grindstones at Gateshead, c. 1920. The local sandstone was particularly suitable for this purpose.*

112. *Consett Iron Company's works, at Consett in County Durham in 1922.*

RUINS OF FURNESS, Stanhope Dene

113. *Apart from the spelling, this old photograph shows the last remains of an iron furnace built just outside Stanhope in Weardale in 1845. It was short-lived and soon replaced by iron works at Tow Law.*

ULLATHORNE & CO

- Manufacturers & Factors -

WORKS BARNARD CASTLE ENGLAND

CHES { PARIS · MELBOURNE & SYDNEY } HEAD OFFICE, 7 to 11, Gate Street, LONDON · W · C

115. *Mrs Lough of Chapman Hill Farm, Witton-le-Wear, a well-known Durham quilter. See also plates 89 and 90.*

114. *A packing label from Ullathorne's Mill, Barnard Castle about 1880. Comparison with plate 110 will show several examples of artist's licence! The mill has been lengthened and raised, and added to at the rear and a non-existent railway has been brought in!*

116. *South Shields old Town Hall, built in 1768, and the adjoining market probably photographed in about 1890.*

117. *Bridgegate in Barnard Castle, probably about 1900. The last of this street was demolished in the early 1950s; it dated back mostly to the eighteenth century, though parts were undoubtedly older.*

118. *Old shops in Gateshead in about 1880.*

119. *A horse-tram in South Shields in about 1900. Horse-trams began running here in 1882 and were replaced by an electric system in 1906.*

120. *The opening of the Darlington tramway system in June 1904.*

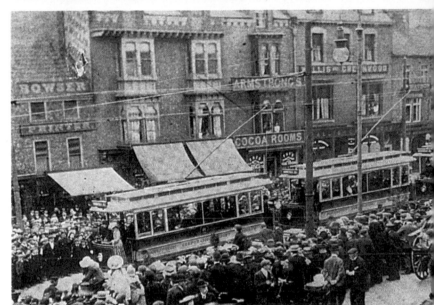

121. *Albert Road, Middlesbrough, in the late 1920s.*

122. *Barnard Castle Market Place decked out to welcome the North-Eastern Cycle Meet in 1909.*

123. *A South Shields bicycle and toy shop at the beginning of the century.*

124. *A soda water carrier in the early years of this century.*

125. *A horse-drawn removal van, probably about 1920, in West Hartlepool.*

126. *A butcher's shop in Sunderland in the early 1930s.*

127. *A knife-grinder in a side steeet, probably in Middleshrough, ahout 1930.*

128. *Co-operative stores flourished in the North-East in the early years of the century and this one at Ashington was probably typical.*

LIFE AND LEISURE

129. *The Jarrow Crusade took place in October 1936 when unemployed shipyard men set out on a 270 mile march to London to ask the government to provide work for their dying town.*

130. *A soup kitchen at Ryhope, County Durham, during the 1926 General Strike.*

131. *A dancing bear, probably at St John's Chapel in Weardale around 1900.*

132. *Brass bands were very popular around the turn of the century and many collieries had their own bands, such as this one in County Durham.*

133. *Cycling as a hobby became popular in the 1890s and outings such as this would take place on a variety of machines then available.*

134. *The humour of fifty years ago often seems very un-funny to us, but doubtless provided much enjoyment at the time.*

135. *Bathing belles of 1913 on the north-east coast.*

136. *Who's for tennis? Probably near Hartlepool at the beginning of this century.*

137. *Funeral cortège at South Shields, about 1910.*

138. *Ena Carter of Trimdon in her pram in 1905.*   139. *A kern baby from the harvest-time of 1905 at Whalton near Morpeth.*

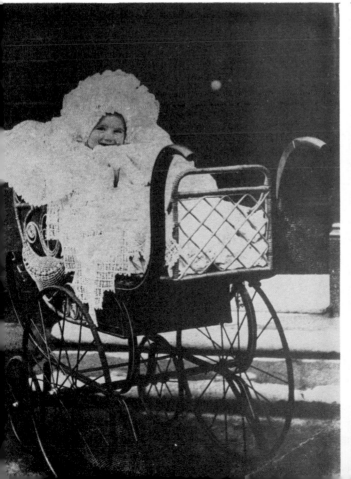 

140. *The Baal Fire ceremony, performed at Whalton, a village near Morpeth, in 1905.*

141. *Tommy Armstrong (1848–1919) of Tanfield Lea, County Durham can truly be called the bard of the Durham coalfield. He was one of the most remarkable of all working-class song-writers.*

142. *A harvest festival thanksgiving at Bothal in Northumberland, 1894.*

agriculture for mining, where they got more money and worked shorter hours, they still kept pigs and poultry. These people always had sides of bacon and hams stored in their houses, together with plenty of fresh eggs. Pig-killing day was an event, and all the neighbours joined in, helping to boil the water necessary for soaking the pigskin after the killing and with the making of black pudding, sausages and potted meat. This slaughter would be carried out in the street and was watched by anyone who might be interested. 'We used to say', recollects Mr Bell, 'that everything was used for food except the pig's squeak.' American bacon was then five pence a pound and Danish eggs twenty four for a shilling.

Many miners kept goats for there was always plenty of open ground and road-sides for grazing, as well as space on the fells. At Cornsay in particular this was very common, though there were also plenty at Evenwood, Cockfield and Butterknowle.

It was said that goat's milk was richer than cow's milk and a goat was certainly a good forager and cheap to keep. The milk was fine in tea and Mr Bell recollects that the families who used this milk were always healthy and took no harm from managing without cow's milk. It was used in all sorts of ways, for cooking as well as for drinking. At Cornsay Colliery there was a pub whose owner also kept goats and was quite an expert on them. Some of his customers had whisky or rum 'watered' with goats milk; this was said to be a fine mixture which did not give a bad head the next morning.

PERSONAL HABITS

Most houses would have a spittoon, a hollow bowl of cast iron or pottery filled with sawdust, for the use of the smokers in the house. The man who smoked at that time did not swallow his spittle when smoking his pipe, but expectorated nearly all the time he was smoking. His pipe would probably be a clay one bought at two for a penny and the tobacco he smoked would be thick twist at threepence an ounce cut off the roll, and of very strong flavour. Some briar pipes were used, but not many, since they soon turned foul and became too wet to smoke comfortably. Some miners took a delight in dyeing their pipes and the man who had the most evenly coloured dark brown pipe was greatly admired. A man who had a meerschaum dyed in this way was the envy of his neighbours and friends. His pipe would be only for special occasions, for parties and when dressed up. These pipes were fairly costly, perhaps up to fifteen shillings or one pound each and quite a number of miners had these pipes which they kept in pipe cases since they were liable to be easily broken.

Sometimes churchwarden pipes would be used when five or six people gathered together for company in the evening. These pipes would be provided by the host, as well as the shag tobacco smoked on such occasions. This would be a gathering of special friends who met occasionally for an evening's chat and sometimes something in connection with their outside interests. It was also the custom to light such a pipe by putting the head to the fire when sitting on the longsettle by the fire. Matches were not then struck commonly, though they were only threepence for a dozen boxes.

Smoking was not allowed down the mine except in very shallow outcrop pits, hence tobacco chewing was a habit practised by the majority of underground workers. Mr Bell recollects seeing young men chewing it all shift and it was said of some that they even ate their bait (food) 'with the chew in their cheek'. There was a special form of tobacco which was very thin like a piece of cord and called 'Ladies Twist'. Of course thick twist and thin twist were commonly used and cost about threepence an ounce. Tobacco chewing is still carried on today, but only by a minority of miners.

It was a common sight when walking round a pit village on a fine evening to see a number of old women smoking clay pipes. If such a lady had a husband they usually sat together on the doorstep, or on chairs, one each side of the door. It was not done whilst walking about or in public and was said to be on doctor's orders as a remedy for 'windy spasms'.

Another practice much used was having one's drinks 'chalked on the slate'. If a man ran out of money when drinking the landlord kept a slate on which the debt would be chalked. This was usually cleared off on the fortnightly pay day. Some men kept this up all the time, always a fortnight in hand and of course the landlord had his own interests to watch, though sometimes he would be caught out. Some landlords would rather give a man a free drink than allow them to chalk it up as this often led to bad debts and loss of custom.

Women did not frequent public houses and most pubs had a special little place called a hatch for the sale of drink which was cheaper when consumed off the premises. Many miners liked their pint at home and their wives would fetch a quart or three gill cans from the nearest pub.

Most elderly men had long shaggy beards and some of these had never been shaved. Some old men had beards down to their waists and it covered most of their chests as well. Beards like this were said to prevent bad chests and sore throats and Mr Bell recollects being told by some old miners that they claimed never to have had a cold in their chest or throat on account of their beards.

A busy and important man of that time was the village barber—they were not called hairdressers then. Safety razors were not in existence and most miners depended upon the barber for shaving. The barber would cut hair from Monday to Thursday but Friday and Saturday he reserved for shaving and it was quite common to see three or four lather boys being engaged whilst the barber followed up with his cut-throat razor shaving off the whiskers, often a week's growth. The charge was a penny for a shave and twopence for a haircut.

Some men cut each other's hair and the horse keeper at the colliery had a fair trade with his horse shears since style was often of little consequence. Miners who did try to shave themselves often cut and marked their chins due to shaving with blunt razors or unsteady hands. The introduction of the safety razor finished that part of the barber's trade and hairdressing has boomed since. It was often said that some barbers used a basin on the head and just cut the hair around the edge as it projected beneath the basin.

Moustache cups were commonly in use then, to prevent a man's moustache being drenched when drinking. These cups had a strip of pottery across the top on which the moustache rested and was kept clear of the liquid. Nearly all men had a moustache at that time, the thicker and heavier the better. One was not supposed to be a man then unless one had some form of moustache or beard. Men often took great pride in their moustaches, having them neatly trimmed with long or short waxed ends set at all sorts of angles, some even at rightangles, and others let them grow thick and bushy without wax.

12 Life in other Industries

Unlike the coal industry, which was quite a logical development for the North-East, the chemical industry seems an unusual one to have been found here. Today there is an enormous chemical manufacturing complex around Billingham and the mouth of the River Tees, but this is a relatively recent development, and the earlier industry began on the banks of the River Tyne during the late 1700s.

At that time, at the beginning of what is often called the Industrial Revolution, the rural population of Britain began to move away from agriculture into the urban areas which were beginning to be engaged in manufacture. This great change was mainly the result of the invention and improvement of the steam engine and the application of mechanisation to the making of textiles, particularly cotton. But this was not the whole of the story, for increased cloth output called for increased quantities of soap, bleach and dyes. And a little later glass too began to be used as a cheap packaging material, especially for drinks and for patent medicines, and the growing factories required more and more cheap window glass.

These several needs of the manufacturing and urban activities can be simplified to a need for one section of the chemical industry—the alkali trade. The importance of alkali can be seen from the following abbreviated statements:

Alkali and fat produce soap
Alkali and sand and lime produce glass.

If one now takes a step still further back into the history of the North-East, one finds that salt was being produced near the mouth of the Tyne in large quantities in the early 1700s. Seawater was boiled in big shallow iron pans and evaporated off to leave salt. Coal was cheap, since only the best coal was evaporated, so this region was particularly well suited to make cheap salt. This production, while good for the manufacturers, was hardly beneficial for those who worked at the salt pans or lived nearby. A visitor to South Shields in 1725 wrote: 'This is the chief place for making salt. The houses here are poor little low hovels, and we are in a perpetual thick nasty smoke.' About that same time Daniel Defoe visited

Newcastle and noted the salt pans which, he said, 'are at Shields, seven miles below the town (i.e. Newcastle); but their coals are brought chiefly from the town. It is a prodigious quantity of coals which those saltworks consume; and the fires make such a smoke, that we saw it ascend in clouds over the hills, four miles before we came to Durham, which is at least sixteen miles from the place'. So pollution of the atmosphere is no new feature of manufacturing towns!

Another industry which came north on account of cheap coal was the glass industry. During the seventeenth century when fears began to grow concerning the destruction of the oak forests for charcoal, those industries which used charcoal as a fuel began to seek other processes and other fuels. One result was that the glass industry moved to the banks of the Tyne, and a little later, to the mouth of the River Wear. As long ago as 1615 it was said of a glass manufacturer from the Isle of Purbeck that 'he was enforced for his last refuge contrary to all men's opinion to make triall at Newcastle upon Tyne where after the expence of many thousand pounds that worke for window-glasse was effected with Newcastle Cole'. Probably the North of England Development Council, busily engaged in encouraging modern industry to come north, experiences similar incredulity about what the region has to offer, until the industrialists have been persuaded to sample its worth.

We have already seen that glass makers needed not only a cheap fuel, but alkali and sand and lime. The two latter were ready to hand in the region and additionally good quality sand was brought cheaply by the colliers, when they returned to the Tyne with it as ballast. So as the glass industry flourished on the Tyne, the demand for alkali grew and so the chemical industry began.

> *When Aa came to Walker work*
> *Aa had ne coat or ne pit sark*
> *Noo Aa's getten two or three;*
> *Walker Pit's deun well for me.*

Walker Pit, as this old song suggests, indeed did well for everyone. Its owners, the Liddells of Ravensworth, were able not only to sell its coal, but also to pump out and sell a concentrated brine from a spring in one of its shafts. From this salt soda was produced and early last century the company was advertising 'Alkali salts, chrystals of mineral alkali, dried chrystals of alkali, barilla salts, chrystals of dried potash and pearl ashes of the usual strength, as are now used in large quantities at the works established near Newcastle, from whence plate, flint and crown glass manufacturers and bleaches may be supplied with the article that suits their purpose.'

Waste disposal began to be a problem as the chemical manufacturing processes grew and a way to deal with one particular evil-smelling waste was found, in the production of 'hypo' which could be used by the paper trade. Hence began the encouragement of another northern industry—paper making.

Yet another and still more dangerous waste product was hydrochloric acid which escaped as poisonous fumes to blight the countryside. A Tyneside manu- facturing firm wrote to a local complainant in the middle of last century: 'Sir, we have received yours of the 16th inst., and are sorry that you should again have reason to complain of damage from our works. We have . . . been at con- siderable pains and expense in putting up condensing apparatus . . . and from our great anxiety to do this very effectually we have made our apparatus of double the extent of Messrs. Attwood & Co's in order that no gas might be suffered to escape into the chimney.' Gas did of course escape until an Act of Parliament made it an offence.

The magnitude of the problem can be judged from a simple chemical calculation: for every ton of salt decomposed about twelve and a half hundredweights of acid gas fell upon the neighbourhood. In 1863 alone for instance the consumption of salt was about 100,000 tons, so more than 60,000 tons of acid gas was liberated. All this is summed up in a dialect song called 'The Changes on the Tyne':

> *Baith sides of the Tyne, aw remember,*
> *Were covered wi' bonny green fields.*
> *But now there is nought but big furnaces.*
> *Down frae Newcastle to Shields.*
>
> *And what wi' their sulphur and brimstone,*
> *Their vapour, their smoke and their steam,*
> *The grass is all gaen, and the farmers*
> *Can nowther get butter or cream.*

The earliest attempts made to get rid of these poisonous fumes took the form of very tall chimneys, which were a prominent feature of the old alkali works, and which are commemorated in further verses of the same song:

> *For making their salts and their soda,*
> *They formerly used a kail-pot,*
> *Wi' an awd-fashioned bit of a chimley*
> *They were quite satisfied wi' their lot.*

> *But now, Anty Clapham, the Quaker*
> *Has filled a' the folks wi' surprize,*
> *For he's lately set up a lang chimley*
> *Within a few feet o' the skies.*

> *There's Losh's big chimley at Walker*
> *Its very awn height makes it shake.*
> *And if Cookson's again tumble over,*
> *It will make a new quay for the Slake.*

But high as such chimneys might be, they could do little to mitigate the situation, for hydrochloric acid gas is readily absorbed by water and so it soon collected into water droplets which fell upon the whole countryside. Its effect on both the lungs of those who breathed it, and upon the surrounding vegetation can be imagined.

Yet the manufacturers, besieged by complaints, fought back. One manufacturer wrote a letter to the press in 1860, which was headed 'Is hydrochloric acid a cure for consumption?' Part of the letter must speak for itself: 'The foreman of the upper works had a lodger, a young man, by trade a ship carpenter, who was very ill and much reduced, evidently in a consumption. One fine day he asked leave to go up in the barge to the upper works, where he remained while the barge was being loaded, all the time breathing an atmosphere highly charged with hydrochloric acid gas. He experienced great relief from this, and often repeated his visit. He regained strength rapidly, so that he was soon able to walk to the works, so eventually I gave him employment there and he became a strong robust workman.'

Although the Alkali Act of 1863 sought to reduce this problem, in the end it was the realisation by manufacturers that the acid represented a financial asset, which finally led them to solve the problem of condensing the noxious gas.

As for the workers, their health must frequently have suffered, their work could be arduous and unpleasant, and it is surprising what little evidence they have left of their way of life. At the peak of its prosperity the Tyneside chemical trade gave direct employment to 10,000 workers, but though keelmen and pitmen are remembered in song and story, little is remembered of the furnace-men, the bleach-packers and the potmen.

Many of those workers were Irish immigrants whose arrival created housing problems. So many factory owners put up rows of small cottages, often described as 'model cottages for working men and their families'. Naturally one could hardly expect such model cottages in the middle of last century to have sanitary fittings, but one notes that in 1845 the Felling Chemical Works made it known that 'aware of the difficulties in small dwellings of securing personal cleanliness which is so valuable an aid to healthy life, they have had baths erected where, for a moderate charge, the worker might go and have a hot bath and cold plunge after it if he so desire'.

By their own light, the alkali masters had a sense of public duty and many were active in the Reform Movement, and provided schools and recreational facilities for the men and their families. Equally, the men seem to have been loyal to their masters, and to have had almost a tribal sense of belonging to a factory. Often grandfathers, fathers and sons would work for the same firm. And on occasions the men would band together to demonstrate their loyalty. In 1843, for example, when the South Shields firm of Cookson's was being heavily prosecuted for damage to crops and pasture, their workmen held a grand procession to the Town Hall to enlist public sympathy for their employers. One of their number, apparently a man of great stature and robust health named Roby, was exhibited as a living proof of the beneficial effects of the atmosphere at the works.

In 1916, Mr Frank Ward of Saltwell, Gateshead, wrote the following verses which demonstrate his attachment to a particular factory (in this case the Friar's Goose Works):

'O give me back my boyhood's days
Those far off days of yore,
When I romped about the Goose Pit Yard
And played on Tyne Main Shore.

'How oft I'd slip the factory gate
When I heard old Bravey snore!
And rush Tom Shannon's ugly stick
To gain the Ball House floor.

'Old Jimmy Boyle I yet can see
At number six pan door.
And see the black salt boiling up
As he sings of Erin's flower.

'How many hours I've stood and watched
Todd's engine great and grand
Just like a woman possing clothes
With piston rods for hands.

'I'll ever see and ever hear
The blowing of them all
The "Sulphur" and the "Weldon's"
And the pumps behind the wall.

'Alas! alas! that I can see
What can be seen there now
The good old Goose dismantled
And the old hands lost to view.'

Of all the variety of jobs in these old chemical works, that of the bleach packers seems to have been the worst. Like the lime dressers—another unhealthy and unpleasant occupation—they had to work in a chlorine-laden atmosphere with pathetically little protective clothing. The bleach packer wrapped his face in a roll of flannel several yards long, sometimes wore leather goggles and wrapped paper round his trouser legs. He had to shovel the bleaching powder through holes in the floor of the bleach chamber into casks below—a process which took twenty or thirty minutes at a time. In a full shift he would spend a total of about six hours in the bleach chamber.

Yet despite such working conditions, most fatal accidents in the chemical works seem to have been due to non-chemical factors such as fires, bursting boilers and structures collapsing. Though occasionally men fell into soda vats or were overcome by fumes.

Nevertheless such recollections as have been recorded suggest that these chemical works were essentially happy places. Or is it that one tends only to recollect the happier occasions of one's life? Certainly these works were hot and thirsty places. A boy was generally on hand to be sent out to one of the many nearby public houses to fetch a gallon of beer to help his elders through the shift.

Today little remains on the landscape to remind one of this once-flourishing industry. Perhaps the most notable monuments are the waste heaps at Felling and Heworth and a fairly substantial heap can still be seen near the preserved Friar's Goose pumping engine house to the east of Gateshead. Most of the other chemical sites have been built over by the later shipyards. Occasionally, during excavation work for building foundations, coloured strata are observed, demonstrating the sites of old works. For example, Prussian Blue was found when Reyrolles built their new office block at Hebburn. And there are still street names and public house names to jog the observant memory: what about the Alkali Hotel at Jarrow, for instance?

Like the Tyneside chemical industry, the Tyne glass industry has virtually disappeared. On the Wear one glass company remains, now part of an American company, making ovenware and domestic glassware. On the Tyne a large glass-house of huge conical-shaped brickwork stands as a monument to the industry which came north three centuries ago. This is at Lemington, to the west of Newcastle and within this enormous structure, probably built around 1800, glass-blowers would labour at the glowing hot pots of molten glass, dipping in their metal tubes to get a blob of glass which they would then blow to the required shape. Gradually mechanisation ousted much of the skill and by the middle of last century 'pressed-glass' bottles had replaced handblown ones. These, shaped within metal moulds, were cheaper and quicker to produce and of a greater accuracy and constant size and shape. By 1850 there were at least forty bottle works in the North-East, but greater concentration of the industry and further mechanisation, using machines developed abroad, has removed yet another industry from this region.

The Lemington 'cone' is now a scheduled 'Ancient Monument' and happily prized by its present owners, but another historic building which was taken down only a few years ago had survived from the eighteenth century to demonstrate yet one more unusual industry. The Shot Tower at Elswick, on the bank of the Tyne to the south-west of the centre of Newcastle, was one of very few such towers constructed to make lead shot. The top of this elegant tower was gained by way of a spiral staircase constructed up the inner side of the wall and at a height of 175 feet one entered a small room provided with a small furnace and a hoist. Lead was hauled up and melted on the spot. Originally coal was probably used to melt the lead, but in more recent years gas had been piped to the top. The molten lead was then carefully poured through a kind of colander and fell the whole height of the tower in droplets, cooling to form spheres as it did so. At the foot of the tower a tank of water received the shot, thus preventing it becoming damaged and mis-shapen. It was then sieved to provide a graded product.

The shot-making men were known as 'runners' and usually worked in pairs—one at the top and one, the senior man, at the bottom. The man at the top would spend most of his working day up there pouring down molten lead and the man at the bottom would clear the water tank and check sizes of shot. Messages, regarding the next size to be made, were passed up and down with a long piece of string. This method continued to be used right to the very end, when the tower was put out of use in 1951. The men refused to accept the suggestion of a telephone, for said one: 'Ye canna always hear properly on a telephone'. Being a runner was a very specialised job with a considerable tradition behind it. Unfortunately not only has that tradition now gone, but the tower itself was taken down a few years ago, having been found unsafe.

Another industry using lead was that of white lead production which was a substance once used as a base in paint manufacture. Like so many lead industries it was often unhealthy and its huge brick-constructed 'stacks' in which the chemical process took place have now been replaced by glass-lined tanks. Here the process goes on under sealed and well-controlled conditions. In the older lead 'stacks' many thousands of small earthenware pots were filled with strong acetic acid and set side by side on a brick floor in a mass of broken tan (oak bark). Each pot was covered by small strips of thin cast lead. Wooden planks were then placed over the pots and a further layer constructed. When the building had been filled it was left for about six weeks, whilst the tan fermented and produced heat which vapourised the acetic acid. This vapour, together with carbon dioxide from the fermentation, resulted in the formation of lead carbonate, or white lead.

When fermentation had ended the stack had to be dismantled and the working conditions of those stripping out the contents beggar description. Apart from the effects, which are now well-known, of breathing lead fumes, imagine working in an atmosphere saturated in acetic acid. (A quick whiff of a vinegar bottle will give the reader a momentary indication!) Old Joe Bennett, who had laboured outside as a young man recollected the terrible hacking coughs and spluttering of the men as they brought out the powdered white lead and earthenware pots. 'None of them lived to any great age,' he said.

By comparison with these relatively light but dangerous chemical industries, heavy engineering, forging and ship building were hard work but dangerous in a more physical way. And skills, developed by the young worker as he gained experience in his trade or work, could help to keep him from danger. Some skills were extended to a remarkable degree in teamwork, as for example, in forging and as plate 107 shows up to seven or eight men would serially strike with large hammers at the hot metal 'Once you'd learned the rythm it was easy—just hellish hard slog!' remembers an old man from Darlington Forge.

Work out of doors might seem superficially more healthy, but that too could be dangerous and exhausting. Quarrying is now greatly reduced since stone is far too expensive to work for any except the most unusual building purpose, but last century it was still a thriving industry. In particular the North-East has long been well-known for its grindstones, cut from a specially fine and hard-grained gritstone quarried not far from the banks of the Tyne. At one time there was a famous saying: 'The world over you'll find a Scot, a flea and a Newcastle grindstone'. But Bill Lowther of Gateshead must be one of the last men alive who remembers them being quarried and cut. He started work when he was not quite fourteen, just as the first world war began. He went to work at Eighton Banks, just outside Gateshead and worked in the quarries until he retired in 1968, fifty four years later. 'I started work at tuppence an hour, and you had to work till you were twenty one before you got the full rate—tenpence an hour. And labourers got sixpence. We started at six in the morning, till half past four at night, except Monday, and we started at eight then, because they thought you might be in a bad fettle with the booze on a Monday! You had to work hard for your living; if you didn't work, you didn't keep your job—you were pushed out and somebody else in your place.'

Although some of the stone around Gateshead was good for building and for grindstones, not all of it was. 'There's fifty feet of what we call 'Rag' on at Spring-well, before you come to the main rock' said Bill, and he explained that by Rag, he meant a rock not good enough for building purposes, so it was broken up for roadmaking. 'But when you got to the stone, it was all naturally flat stuff, maybe nine inches or a foot thick and they used to make little grindstones out of it. Further down you came to the big panels.' By this he meant the solid thick beds of hard stone.

Bill Lowther then went on to explain the way in which these thick beds were quarried. 'On the main rock, if you wanted to cut off the face, you put holes about two feet apart, two inches diameter and when you got them drilled to where you thought the bottom of the panel was, you had to put a reamer in—that was like a flattened drill, but it didn't revolve, it hammered down and made a groove down each side of the hole. Then you charged the hole with gunpowder and got a bit grass and stuffed it down for about eighteen inches, then stemmed it right up to the top of the hole. Then when the powder was lit it flushed up that cut and pushed the stone forward maybe an inch, or two inches—a whole block of stone.'

By this, Bill meant that the block of stone would slide a little, out from the quarry face, moving on a softer bed beneath. 'I've cut a piece forty feet long off the face' he went on, 'and then you had to cut cross-over after that; just big enough for your crane to lift'.

From his description of cutting and making grindstones it was obviously still vivid in his mind: 'After you got out the slab, you put it flat on the banker, put a compass on, and then hammered it round with a square-faced hammer, just to that mark, and once you got that, you had to scappell it down with a quarry pick, using a set square, to make sure you didn't go in under the sides (*i.e.* the cut surface was kept vertical). And when it was halfway down, you got the crane to turn it over and then you hammered that other back. That was the quarryman's job on the banker. The next job was to put a hole in the centre, and then take it down to the lathe and put it on the lathe shaft. The turner used to turn all the rough off it, with a pointed steel bar, and then use a flat tool to plane it'.

Grindstones, as Mr Lowther remembered, were sent all over the world, and they came out of quarries at Springwell, Eighton Banks and Windy Nook—'It was a nice grinding grit at Windy Nook—and scissor makers used to come to the quarry and they'd run their fingers over the stone to make sure of the grit—they didn't want it to hone the scissors, but to cut them.'

'They used to take the big grindstones down to the Felling Shore, on a rolley with horses and a trace horse for Beacon Lough Bank; two horses couldn't get up the Bank without a trace horse to help them up. Sometimes they used to take them onto Newcastle Quay—and load them onto the boats—and then they'd go all over the world—grindstones!'

13 Life in Newcastle

Our concern for the traditions and way of life in the countryside must not blind us to the fact that the social history of the North-East is also closely linked with the development of Newcastle upon Tyne. 'The best designed Victorian town in England and indeed the best designed large city in England altogether', is how Nikolaus Pevsner has described it in his book *The Buildings of Northumberland*. There are of course other important towns and cities in the North-East and Pevsner has again pointed out that the view of Durham Cathedral as one approaches the city on the railway is 'one of the great experiences of Europe' and one must also mention Middlesbrough, grown from four houses in 1812 to a population now approaching quarter of a million. Nevertheless although there are many interesting urban areas in the North-East, Newcastle has clearly been the urban centre of the north and worthy of study on that count alone.

This metropolis of the North was known in the eighteenth century, as we shall shortly see, as an important and elegant city. But in the preceding century its reputation was not always a proud one. Rather than take the views of its inhabitants, let us read the opinions of a series of visitors to the North.

In 1634 three Norwich soldiers, 'a Captain, a Lieutenant and an Ancient, all voluntary members of the noble Military Company in Norwich, agreed to take a view of the Cities, Castles etc. in the Northerne Counties of England'. It was late one August night when they approached 'that Sea-Cole maritime Country Towne', and they had to descend a steep rocky hill; this 'Stony Streete downe to the bridge' being Gateshead. They crossed the Tyne 'by a fayre stone Bridge of 10 Arches with some Towers, to which comes the shipps.' Next day they looked at Newcastle and found 'the people and the streets much alike, neither sweet nor cleane'. Near the cross, however, they found a 'stately prince-like freestone Inne', in which they tasted a cup of good wine, and thus cheered they left for Hexham.

A year later Sir William Brereton of Cheshire travelled through Northumberland and Durham. He had a businessman's view of things and saw at Newcastle 'the fairest quay in England, from Tine-bridge all along the towne-wall and almost to the glassworks'. This, he wrote, is a spacious haven sometimes thronged with ships. He nominated Mr Carre's inn as the fairest built in England, though he lodged at the Swan and paid 8d.

In 1677 Thomas Kirk from Yorkshire journeyed into Scotland and one Thursday night in May he reached Newcastle. Next day he saw St Nicholas Church and a grave 'made for a poor alderman of the town—old Milbank. . . . Our landlord being a wine merchant treated us in his cellar. In the afternoon we went down the river, where we had an abundance of rain, and were wet through the kilt.' The city seems to have made little further impression on him.

Twenty one years later Celia Fiennes, the daughter of a Cromwellian colonel, felt differently. To her, Newcastle 'is a noble town tho' in a bottom. It most resembles London of any place in England, its buildings lofty and large of brick mostly or stone; the streetes are very broad and handsome and very well pitch'd and many of them with very fine Cunduits of water in each, always running into a large stone Cistern for every bodyes use. There is one great streete where in the Market crosse there was one great Cunduit with two spouts which falls into a large Fountaine paved with stone. . . . There is a noble building in the middle of the town all of stone, for an Exchange on stone pillars severall rows; on the top is a building of a very large Hall for the judges to keep the assizes for the town; there is another roome for the Mayor and Councill.' Celia Fiennes goes on to describe St Nicholas Church and then mentions that 'the shops are good and are of distinct trades, not selling many things in one shop as is the custom in most country towns and cittys; here is one market for Corne and another for Hay. Saturday is their biggest Market day . . . it is like a faire for all sorts of provision and goods and very cheape: 2 pence a piece good large poultry; here is leather, woollen and linnen and all sorts of stands for baubles. They have a very indifferent sort of cheese: little things black on the outside and soft sower things'.

In 1724 when Daniel Defoe travelled North he was less interested in food and markets than in the business prospects of Newcastle. It was, he wrote, a spacious extended and infinitely populous place, and he went on to refer to 'a very noble building called the Exchange'. Having mentioned other public buildings and the longest and largest quay to be seen in England (except that of Yarmouth) he went on to complain that the rest of the town to the landward 'is exceeding unpleasant, and the buildings very close and old, standing in the declivity of two exceeding high hills, which, together with the smoke of the coals, makes it not the pleasantest place in the world to live at.'

Jane Harvey made 'A Sentimental Tour' through Newcastle in 1794 and this time it was the inhabitants which caught her attention. Of the monument of the late Alderman Ridley she observed: 'the workmanship is excellent, but the inscription which is much more deeply engraven on the hearts of his fellow-burgesses will be ever a lasting monument of his virtues.' The assembly Rooms 'though smaller than those of York or Bath are not inferior, . . . striking proof of the taste and judgement of Mr Newton, Architect.' At the Hospital for Lunatics 'the patients are treated with all the humanity and attention their unhappy situation can possibly admit', and at the Bridewell 'the prisoners are allowed two-pence per day; the keeper has no salary but the profits of the prisoners' work'. As to some of the streets, 'Mosley-street, so called after the worthy alderman of that name, and Dean-street, both of which have been made within these 9 years, are very great improvements to Newcastle'. The old bridge, which Celia Fiennes, Sir William Brereton and Daniel Defoe described, was now gone, swept away in the great flood of 1771. The new bridge, seen by Jane Harvey, was built in 1780, five arches on the north side belonging to Newcastle, and three to the south belonging to the See of Durham: 'It is rather narrow, being only 22 feet and a half broad; it was the wish of the Corporation to have made it seven feet broader, but the bishop of Durham would not agree to it.'

When able to make their own decisions, the burgesses of Newcastle could on occasion excel in city development, and the period from 1770 to 1840, which has been described as Newcastle's golden age, was undoubtedly a time of great developments. Not only were there silversmiths, designers, engravers on wood (such as Thomas Bewick) and painters on glass (such as the Beilby family), but classical architects such as William Newton who designed the Assembly Rooms in 1776, David Stephenson who designed the early Theatre Royal in 1788, and Mosley Street which was the first new street to be laid out through the old city. William Stokoe was another, and he designed the Moot Hall in 1810, with its Greek Doric portico (Pevsner describes it as possibly the first really Grecian public building in England).

In the early years of the nineteenth-century this 'golden age' reached its brightest period, for it was then that Richard Grainger began his great work. He was only twenty-two when he built a delightful little group of Georgian houses at Higham Place in 1819 (now alas destroyed apart from three houses opposite the Laing Art Gallery).

Grainger indeed began as a small 'speculative' builder, endowed with great energies, but he was fortunate in having the support of the Town Clerk, John Clayton, who was much impressed with Grainger's personality and obviously decided that here was the man who had the determination and organising ability to rebuild the town centre. Richard Grainger was also fortunate in that a group of architects including John Dobson, John Green and his son Benjamin Green with a love and understanding of classical style of building was working in Newcastle at that time. Grainger knew exactly what effects he wanted to achieve, the sort of design he wanted and he employed this rich architectural talent in the planning of his grand design. He was yet again fortunate in being able to build up his own strong team of architects including two men Wardle and Walker who were men of more than ordinary talent.

It was in 1834 that Grainger's detailed proposals for a new Town Centre first appear in the Council minute books. What is almost as impressive as the buildings which he produced, is the speed with which he operated. It is recorded, for example, that on 24th May 1836 Grainger signed a contract with the owners of the old Theatre Royal in Mosley Street to build them a new and beautiful Theatre Royal, and three hours after the contract was signed the chimneys were down and within a day or so the old theatre had disappeared. Would that decisions could be made as clearly and rapidly today and acted upon with equal facility! By June 1837 the new streets of the town centre had been completed and flagged, and the hundreds of shops and houses occupied. In 1838 Benjamin Green's column to Earl Grey was erected providing a dramatic new centrepiece for the whole city. Unfortunately much of Grainger's work has been destroyed in recent years, though very fortunately Grey Street remains. It has been described by Pevsner as 'one of the best streets in England' and, one hopes, is now safeguarded by more sensitive and informed planning control than was available in the 1950s and 1960s.

It is an interesting side issue to note that during the first half of the nineteenth century, it was possible for an architect to turn his hand from designing buildings and monuments to designing civil engineering. Thus Benjamin Green, having designed his emphatic column to Earl Grey at the head of Grey Street, was able, in the same year, to start constructing two remarkable railway viaducts for the Newcastle and North Shields railway. One of these runs across the valley of the Ouseburn and the other across the Willington Dene—a total of sixteen arches, the foundation stones for which were laid in 1837. The abbutments and piers of both these viaducts are of stone, but five of the arches of the Ouseburn bridge and all the seven arches of the Willington Dene bridge were of timber, of a laminated construction which represents practically the first use of that technique in this country.

It is this sense of excitement, of experimentation and of involvement in a variety of activities, which somehow comes through to us from the early nineteenth century in Newcastle. Take for example the many societies, several of them now of national status. The Literary and Philosophical Society had been founded in

1793; then in 1813 both the Antiquarian Society of Newcastle and the Society for Preventing Accidents in Coal Mines were founded. Three more societies came in the 1820s. These were the Northumberland Institution for the Promotion of Fine Arts in 1822, the Horticultural and Botanical Society in 1824 and also the Newcastle Mechanics Institute in that same year. In 1834 the Medical School began, and this was later to be one of the co-founding departments of the University of Newcastle upon Tyne. In 1852 the North of England Institute of Mining and Mechanical Engineers was founded and in 1871 the College of Physical Science came into being. Public discussion about such a college in Newcastle had begun at least as early as 1831 when a paper on the idea was read to the Literary and Philosophical Society. It received powerful support in 1853 after the foundation of the Institute of Mining and Mechanical Engineers, but almost another twenty years of debate and correspondence had to pass before the college was founded. It was this college which later became known as Armstrong College, and which eventually, along with the medical college, became two departments of the University of Durham and still later the fully independent University of Newcastle upon Tyne.

So far we have viewed the City of Newcastle through the eyes of visitors and some of its more worthy citizens. Let us finally look at it from the viewpoint of one of its more everyday citizens. Around the beginning of this century Jack Common lived in fairly squalid housing in the Byker area to the east of the City. He wrote two novels, *Kiddar's Luck* and *Ampersand* which have belatedly become 'accepted' and into these he poured much of himself and his life in those busy tram-rattled gas-lit streets before the first world war:

'From St Peter's you looked down a hillside of staggered roofs and cobbled streets to where the river slid like new-boiled pitch under ships and quays until it took the glitter of the lights on several bridges, high and low, or writhed with reflected flame as a train passed over. That was the basic scene, but as you descended, its angles and emphasis shifted. Bridges moved their relation to one another; quays and the shipping flattened out, losing the river behind them; and the centre of the town began to rise up. Then on the river-side itself, when you were near enough to smell its dankness and the touch of salt that blew up from it and to see its scum of corks and contraceptives and half-wrecked crates washing under the sterns of foreign ships, the bridges were now high overhead. You saw, too, that it was a fortress-city you were making for. There was a climb ahead of you before you got into the inner gaiety of crowds. Either you toiled up Dean Street, which was a sort of glacier of asphalt and cobblestones coming down steeply and ponderously by a cliff of office buildings and through a black railway arch before it could spread itself out on an easier gradient; or you could try your wind and leg-muscles on the Dog Leap Stairs, in which latter case you emerged just where the old keep of the original 'new' castle sits in its breast-high mesh of shining railway-lines.'

'. . . the naptha-lit stalls of the Bigg Market. A fascinating assembly of highly-coloured hucksters then filled the acre of cobbles in front to the Town Hall. The press of people coming into it became instantly ruddy-faced and bright-eyed as the naphtha-flares fanned out, eating the air just overhead, their smoke visibly coiling up to a brazen sky. Yet the confusion of light and smoke was almost outdone by the competitive racket of cries and spiels going up from all those stalls. The beauty of it was that all this vocalized salesmanship was concerned with giving stuff away. A fellow with leather lungs and a straw hat ceaselessly compiled huge bags of confectionery, which he proceeded to give away (except that as a matter of form he took a shilling back each time) right and left and three rows back of the crowd. Next to him a herbalist, hoarse as a crow, logically recommended his cough candy as invaluable and practically costless. Rival ice-cream wagons, their gilt and cream and blue almost a coloratura cry on the lit air, echoed to Italian-tinted Tyneside as their crews of brisk dark men flung bigger and bigger dollops into brass sandwich-makers and unhesitatingly let the public know exactly what was being given away to them. There were whelk-stalls, scent-stalls, fruit-stalls, drink-stalls, clothing-stalls, all advertising vocally this fever of Saturday philanthropy they all shared.'

'. . . the Bird Market. An incredible joint, that. It stood on a corner above the Fish Market, which by the time I got there would be dead except for cleaners swilling water around behind its iron grilles. But upstairs, the Bird Market windows were fairly at bursting-point with a fullness of smoky light. A narrow staircase led up to this place, and so many people were coming and going upon it, you would find yourself halted on one foot before the other could get a toe-hold between several sets of heels. What lived at the top of them was a sort of sweet-noted pandemonium. The walls were hung with tiers of cages, most of them tiny, which contained a various flutter connected with canaries, linnets, and the finches, bull, gold or green, all singing madly so as to get themselves sold quick. From tier to tier layers of smoke thick as felt, stretched and sagged or floated. Under and in that smoke were the bird-fanciers, most of them pitmen, as you could see whenever they removed their caps to scratch their heads and the blue coal scars showed up. They all smoked, they all spat, they all swore. And they did these things faster when a knot of them gathered together in wonder before a bird that really was a mazer. How they could hear that particular warbler out of all the rest was a mazer to me, but it seemed they could, these connoisseurs of the canary-voice, or, at least, they let on they could, and you can't contradict a pitman.

'There were no women present, in fact, it was doubtful if a woman could have lived in that atmosphere, not for long, anyway.'

14 Dialect and Games

Dialect is by no means dead, though it has suffered greatly, firstly by a century of education and secondly in more recent years by pressures from the BBC. These latter pressures have now eased, and local broadcasting services make use of local speakers in a way which would have been unthinkable in the thirties.

In the same way that we have seen how place-names can help to identify traces of past invaders, so we can observe that dialect, in its pronunciation and vocabulary, has preserved traces of original varieties of the language—the speech of other races—which are not incorporated in Standard English. So do not let us confuse dialect with 'sloppy speech'; rather let us see it as part of our colourful heritage and look for traces of Scandinavian or Norman invaders, discernible in a more subtle way than earthworks and castles, but just as real.

We must, however, also remember that words, unlike place-names, are almost living things and their distribution may demonstrate the added factor of the 'vigour' or the 'popularity' of these words. If we were to make a village by village survey of the countryside and find out where particular dialect words are still used, we would end up with distribution maps like those shown in Fig. 28. These maps are in fact based on a very detailed and thorough dialect survey made over the whole of England by the late Professor Harold Orton (who incidentally was born in County Durham), and his team of workers from Leeds University.

Take the word *slape*, for instance. It means, in standard English, slippery. Fig. 28 (1) is shaded to show where that word is still used, and this is roughly the same as the area of Scandinavian settlement in the ninth and tenth centuries. However, the word *dike,* meaning a hedge, although also of Scandinavian origin, has ceased to be used in Yorkshire though it is still commonly remembered in the Lake District and parts of Durham and south Northumberland. On the other hand some Scandinavian words have not only remained in use in the south, but have gained an extended use in the north, such as *throng,* meaning busy.

Gaumless meaning silly seems to have lost a great deal of popularity except in the hills and parts of Durham and *ket* (rubbish) has yielded in both the north and south, and is now only remembered in a narrow band across parts of Cumberland, Westmorland, south Durham and north Yorkshire.

Of course there are many other words of dialect interest in the north apart from those of Scandinavian origin. Some are peculiar to the North-East, such as *ploat*—to pluck feathers from a dead chicken, which is a Low German borrowing characteristic of north-east England (Fig. 28 (7)). *Bullets* meaning children's sweets and derived from French *boulette* is restricted to Northumberland and Durham, whilst *yeddle* (urine), an Old English word, has a very limited distribution in the Allendale and Upper Weardale hills (Fig. 28 (8)). I recently came across this old word when talking to Mr Jack Grey of Pease's Mires Farm above Stanhope. I was looking at an old pump in his farmyard and asking what he called it. 'A yeddle pump' he said. And what was it used for? . . . 'For pumping yeddle.' Of course! In fact urine from the cowhouses was drained across the yard into a stone underground tank and pumped up from there by hand, as required, into a wooden barrel on the back of a farmcart. This, with its bung knocked out, was then driven back and forth across a field, yielding rich green grass.

So this old word, as with a number of others, is still part of the local vocabulary. But so far we have referred to the words of dialect; what of the pronunciation? This varies considerably even within our relatively limited region of the North-East, and anyone who thinks that the people of the North-East speak some generalised dialect called 'Geordie' should listen to a Northumbrian farmer speaking with that characteristic 'rolling' 'r', then listen to a rapid urban speaker from, say, the Scotswood area of Newcastle, then to a miner from East Durham with his own particular speech, then perhaps to a shepherd from upper Weardale. All these speakers have a lot in common, yet each has his own characteristic tone and accent, as well as variations in dialect words. Equally each of these speakers has preserved something from the many settlers and invaders who have come to this region.

The ordinary reader can, without even collecting these many nuances of speech, gain amusement by a very simple experiment. Ask someone from Sunderland what he asks for when ordering a helping of fish and chips at his local shop. If he was born and bred in Sunderland he will probably ask for 'a fish lot'. Someone from Gateshead would probably ask for 'a paper' and somebody from Stanley in West Durham would probably ask for 'a fish and bag'. And there are other words associated with this delicious food such as 'scraggins' from Shildon. No doubt if this experiment is carried further afield other phrases or words will be found. These are living words and phrases, but with very restricted distribution, and

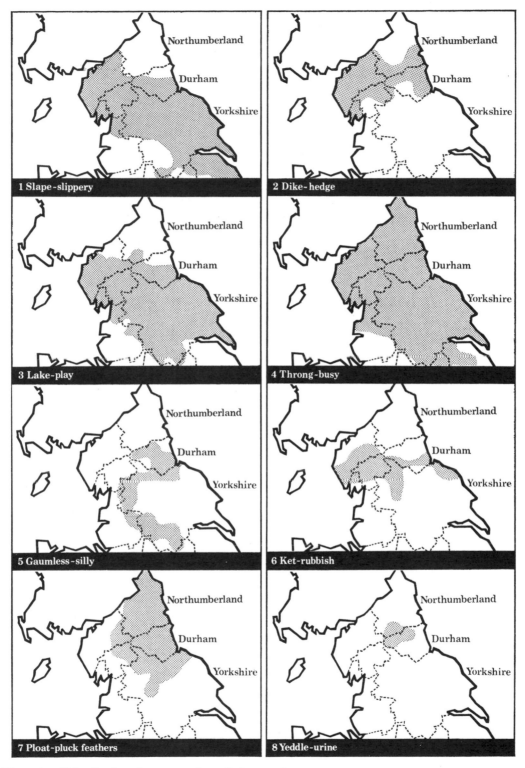

Fig. 28. *Distribution of some northern dialect words.*
These sketch maps are based on A Word Geography of England *by Orton and Wright, and show where old dialect words are still remembered. See page 134.*

quite unknown within a few miles. Clearly they are not of great antiquity (fish and chips probably date from the second half of last century), but they indicate that local variations in speech were still capable of developing even as recently as seventy or so years ago.

Finally one should point out that whilst much of the old dialect vocabulary is being lost from everyday speech, some words are preserved for all time in place-names and in street names and one example may help to make this point.

The word *gate* (pronounced in the North-East rather as 'gey-et') can mean a way, a path, or a street. Many towns have such 'gates' even though they were never walled, and so the word does not really refer to an *entrance*, so much as a way. For example the small town of Barnard Castle nestling close to the castle was never itself walled, but it has Bridgegate (the way to the bridge), Northgate and Galgate (the way past the gallows). And Darlington, another unwalled market town, has Skinnergate, Bondgate, Northgate, Priestgate and Blackwellgate. In the countryside 'gate' can mean a path often trodden by pack horses; for example 'Limersgate' along which burnt lime was taken from the lime kilns of the limestone country. The word has also meant, especially in mining context, a short journey and Rev. F. M. T. Palgrave in *Words & Phrases in everyday use by the Natives of Hetton-le-Hole* wrote in 1896, 'A workman removing a heap of stones, if asked how much still remains, will sometimes answer, "Another gyet'll takd up", meaning one more journey; or "Aa just hev another gyet te gan".' Whilst such a meaning has now almost certainly disappeared from everyday speech, the word is at least preserved in several street names.

SPORTS AND PASTIMES

We tend to forget in these days of mass entertainment, either at the football match, or round the home television set, that fifty years and more ago many men entertained themselves in small groups sometimes as a club and often associated with their local pub. Games such as quoits come to mind, played with heavy metal rings kept shiny with use. Single quoits, for everyday play, might be fashioned out of heavy shire horse-shoes, though a proper set for match playing would be carefully made, with chamfered edges. At the beginning of the match season such a set of quoits might have become rather dull if not actually rusty, but they would be cleaned, someone from Darlington recalled, by being put in the wooden pig trough along with the pig-swill. The rooting around of the pigs would soon have them shiny again!

Pigeon-fancying continues to be very popular and several Durham pit villages still have a colourful array of *crees* nearby. (Incidentally north of the Tyne the word

Fig. 29. Pigeon crees near Chester-le-Street.

for the pigeon hut is a *ducket*, presumably akin to the Scottish word for a dove-cot). As with other deceptively simple occupations there are many intricate 'tricks of the trade', some of which are secretly prized and only passed from father to son. One rather cruel method was observed by Pete Elliott of Birtley, when a pigeon had been given to a child, but insisted on returning to its home roost. After its second return the ex-owner put the pigeon in a big biscuit tin, replaced the lid, and then kicked the tin around his yard a few times. When released the pigeon shot away to its new home without further ado.

Another occupation which not only continues to thrive, but has a great many devotees and much secretly held lore is that of leek growing. Leek Clubs hold annual shows and prizes can be quite valuable including, for example, a colour television set, or a canteen of cutlery. Much bitterness can be generated between growers, and leek-slashing at dead of night to prevent someone winning is not unknown. For this reason some noted leek growers will travel several miles to tend their plants in an unknown allotment and their recipes for enriching the soil are held as dark secrets. Recently we came across a pitman who had just moved out of an old terrace to more modern accommodation, since his old house was about to be demolished. A few nights later he came back to dig out his leek patch of specially concocted soil, only to find a large hole—someone had been there before him and stolen several sackfuls of earth.

Cycling, by contrast, was a communal affair, with a band of men meeting to go on long Saturday jaunts and occasions such as the Whitsuntide Cycle Meet at Barnard Castle were extraordinarily well attended for many years. In more recent years, and now known quite simply as The Meet, it has changed its function to that of a Carnival, and many people have entirely forgotten that its original purpose was for cyclists from many miles around to meet together for a day.

If the cycle club has practically disappeared, many a brass band still prospers. A large number of collieries had their own bands, whose greatest day of the year was probably at the Durham Big Meet—the day when all the pitmen and their families gather for a day at Durham City—for the band would proudly lead the lodge banner into the city and on to the racecourse. As collieries have closed and the communal spirit of many a village has been lost, the bands have died too. But occasionally, as with the Ever Ready Band at Tanfield near Stanley, the colliery band has been kept active, or resuscitated, by an incoming industry.

Handball was a game played by both men and boys. As a man's game it was particularly played in the Durham coalfield and special *alleys* were constructed, often at the back of pubs. Each alley consisted of a solid smooth-surfaced wall some thirty feet long and almost as high, with a good clear area in front. There are a number of such alleys still standing, including one at High Etherley, near the A68 and others at Langley Park behind the Langley Park Hotel, at Leasingthorne behind the Eden Arms, at Eldon Lane behind the Cumberland Arms and at Windy Nook behind the Black Fell Inn.

Several men are still remembered as having been great hand ball players and quite large sums of money were bet on their games. The boys' game was not dissimilar, though generally played against the plain gable end of a house. Mr Ketchen of Jarrow recalls that the gable was roughly marked out in chalk with vertical side boundary lines as high as could be reached and about twenty feet apart, and a base line was chalked about three feet above ground level. The wall play area was that between the side lines and above the base line to any height. Two players took part, using an air-filled ball about three inches in diameter called a tuppenny ball, because that is what it cost. The ball was bounced on the ground, then struck against the wall with the palm of the hand. The other player allowed it to bounce once on the ground and then returned it direct to the wall. This went on, until the ball either landed outside the wall play area or was not

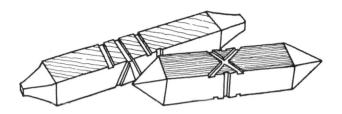

Fig. 30.   Kitty cats.
Small wooden shapes (about three or four inches long) used in a northern children's game. See page 140.

returned on the first bounce, thus ending the *volley* and scoring a point to the other player.

The game, recalls Mr Ketchen, was then restarted and continued until one player had scored twenty-one points as the winner, or until the occupants of the house came out and chased them away because of the thumping of the ball against their wall.

And finally here are two games for children, one predominantly played by boys and the other by girls. Mrs Platt of Heaton near Newcastle remembers, as a child,

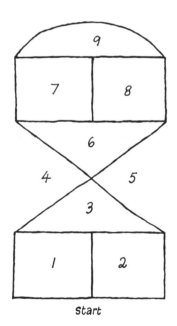

Fig. 31.   Layout of the game of bays.
This pattern was chalked on the pavement and a piece of stone called a dabber was slid from bay to bay.

playing *bays* for many hours on summer evenings. The bays were drawn out on the pavement in chalk and a small flat piece of stone called a *dabber* was slid into first bay (marked with a '1': See Fig. 31). The player hopped into '1', picked up the dabber and went back to start, then hopped into '2' and so on, moving back each time to 'start'. When the '3' bay came up, one could use both feet to cover 1 and 2, but one then had to hop into '3'; similarly both feet could be used in 4 and 5 when going into 6, and on 7 and 8 when going into '9'.

So far, that was the first 'go' and after that it was an all-hopping game and the dabber had to be slid into the right number. If one missed getting it into the right number, one would lose a turn and have to try again.

A boys' game was apparently called *Tip the Cat* around Low Fell near Gateshead and *Kitty Cat* around Bedlington in Northumberland (and perhaps other names elsewhere in the region). To play this a piece of wood about three-quarters of an inch square and four or five inches long was pointed at each end and on each flat side a Roman Numeral was carved: I, II, III and IV or X. The stick was placed on the ground and hit at one end by a striking stick. It would then fly some distance. Mr Clarke of Low Fell remembers that 'if it fell with the cross up, you were finished. On the other hand you got one, two or three knocks (depending on what number showed) and the winner was the one furthest from the starting line'. In Bedlington a more complicated, though basically similar game, was played from a circle about three feet across drawn on the ground. The striker had to hit the cat as it was thrown into the circle, and he had to hit it at least once in three throws, or he would be out. If he did hit it, and it was not caught, he noted the uppermost number when it landed. He then hit it, as it lay on the ground, on one of the pointed ends, and repeated this for the number shown when it had first landed. Then the striker would tell the thrower how many jumps he would offer to make between the ring and the Cat. Depending on whether the challenge was taken up or not, so the score would go. Sometimes the jumps were specified as 'a hop-step and a jump' or as 'jumps backwards', to make it more difficult.

15 Dances, Songs and Customs

THE NORTHERN SWORD DANCE

If, as seems likely, the old folk play of *St George and the Dragon* with its many regional variations, contains traces of a pagan ritual, then the northern sword dance, which can be linked with this same tradition, is a precious relic from the past still lingering with us.

Several folk dances, each with its own scrap of tradition of verse or dress, have been recorded from many parts of England, but had it not been for Cecil Sharp who founded the English Folk Song & Dance Society and himself collected widely and assiduously, many would have been lost. It is very probable that the northern sword dances would have been among those lost, but for the timely collecting by Sharp. More than sixty years ago he recorded fourteen sword dances in northern counties, and of these, nine were from Yorkshire, five of the teams each having six dancers and four of the teams having eight dancers. Each of these nine dances used sets of swords which were roughly three feet long and consequently these Yorkshire dances are usually described as 'long-sword' dances. In the other northern counties he recorded two dance teams from Durham, namely Winlaton and Swalwell and three from Northumberland—Earsdon, North Walbottle and Beadnell.

It is with these latter five dances that we are concerned here. They are generally known as 'rapper' dances or short sword dances, to distinguish them from the longer swords used elsewhere. The sword is about twenty inches long of thin spring steel and has a wooden handle at either end; one of these is usually swivelled to facilitate the complicated dance movements.

There are several differences between the Yorkshire and north-eastern performances, mainly due to the great speed at which the north-eastern dances are performed and the use of the 'rant' step enhances this. The other difference which is perhaps significant about the north-eastern sword dance is that there are five dancers to a team, whereas all the Yorkshire teams require six or eight men.

Of the five teams recorded by Sharp in the early years of this century only one has a continuing tradition, namely the Backworth team (from near Earsdon, Northumberland). It was the Earsdon dance which the painter Ralph Hedley illustrated in a painting now apparently lost, which he made around 1800. A line drawing based on this painting was illustrated in one of Sharp's booklets describing his record of northern dancers. Although this dance tradition was almost lost this century, there are probably now more teams performing than at any time since 1900, due to a revival of teams of young dancers. One notable example is the Newcastle University Team founded by Professor Fisher-Cassie.

All these sword dances are elaborately performed to a complicated series of steps, each performer holding the handles of two adjoining swords. After a series of gyrations and pattern-steps they cross their swords to form a 'lock' or 'nut' and this is held aloft by the leader as a triumphal finale. Although the dance is now the main performance, the five dancers are joined by a captain and a kind of 'fool' known as a Betty or a Bessie, and they are accompanied by a musician playing a fiddle, or sometimes now, as at Earsdon, a piano accordion.

These dances and their ritual performance are all that now remain of a much longer and still more complex ritual, for it seems clear that they are part of what was once a folk-play including a wooden-beamed plough which was borne by the players and known as a stot plough (the word stot is an old dialect word for a young ox: presumably the animal which originally pulled the plough). The performers then acted a short play in which one of their members was ceremonially killed and brought to life again by a doctor. The dance then concluded the whole performance. Plays of this kind, or parts of them, are known throughout this country and many parts of Europe. They are probably fertility rites of some considerable antiquity. Thus the plough itself indicates the dependence upon the fertility of the soil and the character who is ceremonially 'slaughtered' was often dressed with animal skins, making the ceremonial sacrifice of a traditionally important animal still clearer. The 'bringing back to life' part of the play is also significant as representing Spring and the annual rebirth of life. Such plays were often performed in mid-winter, on the first lengthening day which heralded the new year.

It is not without interest in this context to learn that when Cecil Sharp was recording these dances in around 1910 he talked to a Mr Armstrong who was then captain of the Earsdon Sword Dance Team. Mr Armstrong told him that he had danced for forty years with that team before he had retired from an active performance and taken up his position as Captain. He recollected the Bessie as originally wearing a hairy cap and when the 'nut' was about to be tied the dancers would sometimes call out 'We'll hang the Betty' upon which Betty would step into the centre of the ring and the sword would be locked tightly around his throat, whilst the dancers stepped to the completion of the tune. Thus we can see that towards the end of the nineteenth-century the very old play still retained a little more of its original character than it does today.

The costume too has changed and whereas today it is often a fairly simple one with breeches and white shirts, the dress which is shown in Ralph Hedley's painting of about 1880 seems much more elaborate. Hedley assured Cecil Sharp when they met about 1900, that at the time of his painting the dancers wore white shirts decorated with bows and rosettes of coloured ribbons, black breeches of alpaca or satinette, knee ribbons and striped stockings with shoes tied with ribbons. The Bessie was dressed in woman's clothes, with a long skirt and bonnet.

The rappers or short swords which the dancers use as an essential feature of their performance have themselves aroused discussion as to their origin. Indeed there is some doubt as to the origin of the very name 'rapper'. One explanation rests on the fact that when the dancers use the rant step they rap the floor regularly and hence the dance and later, by association, the swords were described by the adjective rapper. It has also been suggested that the name comes from rapier, a slender short sword, but it has also been pointed out that the shape of the present swords and their flexible nature make them likely to have been the instruments originally used for scraping down pit ponies after a day's dirty work underground. Certainly we have come across recollections of elderly pitmen, in charge of underground ponies, who recollect having used something of this kind to scrape off the sweaty dirt from their ponies. However, there is little doubt that although these scrapers or swords may not themselves have a history longer than one or two centuries, the dance is, as a tradition, much older than that and it is pleasant to note that the current performances of the Backworth sword dance team are as lively as ever, and still carried out by pitmen as a part-time occupation. Nevertheless they have polished up their performance to a state where it is frequently demonstrated on many a public stage to the great enjoyment of north-eastern audiences.

SONGS AND BALLADS

It is difficult, on the printed page, to give adequate treatment of the strong north-eastern tradition of song and ballad, and all we can do here is to mention a few of the best-known songs and draw attention to a few of the better-known writers. Without doubt a strong contender for the 'national anthem of the North-East' is *Blaydon Races*. Its success is due to both its rollicking tune and its cheery chorus. The melody was borrowed from a now-forgotten song called *Brighton*, but its words are entirely those of George Ridley, a native of Gateshead. His biography is brief. He was born in 1835 and at the age of eight he was sent to work. In his early twenties he met with a serious accident and was unable to continue in employment. Thereafter he earned a livelihood as a singer of Irish comic and old Tyneside songs, but after a brief but successful career of about five years on the music hall stage his health began to fail and he died at Gateshead in September 1864, aged thirty years.

> *Aw went to Blaydon Races, 'twas on the ninth of Joon,*
> *Eiteen hundred an' sixty-two, on a summer's efternoon;*
> *Aw tyuk the 'bus frae Balmbra's an' she wis heavy laden,*
> *Away we went alang Collingwood Street, that, on the road*
> *to Blaydon.*
>
> *Chorus:*
> *O lads ye shud a' seen us gannin'*
> *Passin' the foaks upon the road just as they wor stanning';*
> *Thor wes lots o' lads an' lasses there, all wi' smilin' faces,*
> *Gannin' along the Scotswood Road, to see the Blaydon Races.*

Another contender for the North-East's 'national anthem' is surely *Keep Your Feet Still Geordie Hinny* written by Joe Wilson (1841–1875), one of the best of the region's song writers and dialect poets. This music hall performer and publican turned temperance reformer died of T.B. in his early thirties. He left his own epitaph; 'It's been me aim to hev a place i' the hearts o' the Tyneside people wi' writin' bits of hyemly songs aw think they'll sing.'

> *Wor Geordy and Bob Johnson byeth lay i' one bed*
> *In a little lodgin' hoose that's doon the shore.*
> *Before he'd been an hour asleep a kick from Geordy's fut*
> *Made him waken up te roar i'steed o' snore.*
>
> *Chorus:*
> *'Keep yor feet still Geordy Hinny*
> *Let's be happy for the neet*
> *For Aa may nit be se happy thro' the day,*
> *So give us that bit comfort, keep yor feet still Geordy lad*
> *And divvent drive me bonny dreams away.*

Tommy Armstrong (1848–1919) of Tanfield Lea can truly be called the bard of the Durham coalfield and one of the most remarkable of all working-class song-writers. He was a small lively bow-legged man, 'cursed with fourteen children and a bottomless thirst' (as his eldest son said). Little money would be left out of his miner's wages for his own pleasures and so he made songs, had them cheaply printed and sold these broadsides round the pubs at weekends, a penny a time, to raise beer-money. His son William once said: 'Me dad's muse was a mug of ale'.

When young, Armstrong earned local fame as a ballad-maker and he was looked to to make a song on any important event in the life of the mining community such as a strike or a pit-disaster. He was very conscious of his responsibilities and is on record as saying: 'When ye're the Pitman's Poet an' looked up to for it, wey, if a disaster or a strike goos by wi'oot a sang fre ye, they say: "What's wi' Tommy Armstrong? Has someone druv a spigot in him an' let oot aal the inspiration?" Me aud sangs hev kept me in beer, an' the floor o' the public bar hes bin me stage for forty year. Aw'd sing, we'd drink, aw'd sing, we'd drink agen, sangs wi'oot end, amen.'

Perhaps his best known song is *Durham Jail* inspired, it is said, because he found himself in gaol. It was alleged that he had helped himself to a pair of pit stockings in West Stanley Co-op. He said he was 'elevated' at the time and, the way the stockings were displayed, they seemed to him the only pair of bow-legged ones he'd ever seen and in his condition he couldn't resist them.

When ye gan inte Durham Gaol
They'll find ye with employ,
They'll dress ye up se dandy
In a suit o' corduroy;
They'll fetch yer a cap wivoot a peak,
An' niver ax yor size,
An' like yor suit it's corduroy,
An' it comes doon ower yor eyes.

Chorus
O there's ne good luck in Durham Gaol,
There's ne good luck at aal;
What's bread an' skilly for,
But just te make ye smaal?

One of the most moving little songs to me is by some unknown writer: *Jowl and Listen*. A local headmaster, Walter Toyn of Whickham, collected this song from Henry Nattrass of Low Fell. In its broad accent, described by miners as 'pitmatic', it tells how an experienced pitman warns a raw recruit at the coal face how to find out whether the coal is secure by striking (jowling) it with his pick haft before beginning to hew.

Chorus
Jowl, jowl and listen, lad,
Ye'll hear that coalface workin,
There's mony a marra missin', lad,
Because he wadn't listen, lad.

Me father aalwes used to say,
Pit-wark's mair than hewin',
Ye've got te coax the coal alang,
An' not be rivin' an' tewin'.

Chorus
Jowl, jowl etc. . . .

Noo the deppity craals from flat te flat,
An' the putter rams the tyum uns, (empty ones, i.e. empty coal
   tubs)
An' the man at the face must knaa his place,
Like a mother knaas her young uns.

Chorus
Jowl, jowl etc. . . .

All these examples make clear that folklore traditions were strong among the
north-eastern miners and it is surely no accident that even today, among these
miners, there are some of the finest sword dancers in Europe, with a tradition
that could well stretch back to the earliest days of mining in England.

The folk music dialect of the North-East is a distinctive one, probably affected
by the peculiarities of the Northumbrian pipes. A. L. Lloyd, an authority on this
subject, maintains that many of the earlier melodies of our region show this bag-pipe
character clearly. But gradually, through the nineteenth-century, the writing of
melodies in the local tradition dwindled among the miners. For the growth of
other industries such as engineering, shipbuilding and so on brought intensive
urbanisation and in consequence the rapid growth of the vaudeville theatre.
From this came, for example, the popular songs we have just seen: *Blaydon Races*
and *Keep your Feet Still*. Perhaps the miner's song repertory would have become
completely urbanised in this way had not an influx of Irish labourers begun, which
persisted for several years. The great Irish Potato Famine of 1845–52 sent them
pouring across and with them came a rich stock of native melody. This merged
with the existing north-eastern repertory and had the effect of restoring its 'folk'
character, just as it was beginning to fade. Tommy Armstrong, Lloyd believes,

was influenced by both the stage and the newly revived folk song. He had a great liking for the Irish-style tunes so popular in the coalfield towards the end of the last century and in particular for that genre called the 'come-all-ye'.

Today we are witnessing yet another revival and though it may be invidious to select names of current singers, one might mention Ed Pickford whose songs are usually grave and who is particularly noted for: *Ee, Aye, Aa cud hew*:

When aa was young and in me prime,
Ee, aye, aa cud hew.
Well, aa was hewin' aall the time.
Now me hewin' days are through, through,
Now me hewin' days are through.

And surely Alex Glasgow, that humorous, bitter yet witty satirist who wrote the title song for the musical play *Close the Coalhouse Door* will also take his place in the folk song history of the North-East:

Close the coalhouse door, lad
There's blood inside;
Blood from broken hands and feet,
Blood that's dried on pit black meat,
Blood from hearts that know no beat;
Close the coalhouse door, lad
There's blood inside.

Close the coalhouse door, lad
There's bones inside;
Mangled splintered piles of bones,
Buried 'neath a mile of stones,
Not a soul to hear the groans;
Close the coalhouse door, lad
There's bones inside.

Close the coalhouse door, lad
There's bairns inside;
Bairns that had no time to hide,
Bairns that saw the blackness slide,
Bairns beneath the mountainside;
Close the coalhouse door, lad
There's bairns inside.

CUSTOMS RELATING TO BIRTH, MARRIAGE AND DEATH

Many customs, of which we can still identify traces today, have a surprisingly long antiquity. Some two centuries ago when 'antiquarianism' was popular John Brand, himself a northerner, brought together many published references to customs, ceremonies and superstitions and added to these some of his own observations. In his Preface he wrote:

'I shall offer many Discoveries which are peculiarly my own, for there are not a few Customs yet retained in the North, where I spent the earliest part of my life, of which I am persuaded the learned in the Southern parts of our Island have hardly once heard mention, which is perhaps the sole cause why they have never before been investigated.'

It is all the more satisfying when one discovers still just alive today some custom or ceremony in virtually the same form that Brand observed it. For it is quite likely that everyday customs, as recorded two centuries ago, were but little different from what they had been in medieval times. It is over the last hundred and thirty years when tremendous population movements as well as social changes have taken place, that cultural loss has been greatest. Hence to discover some habit or custom today which is similar to that described by John Brand, is probably to take oneself back many centuries. Whilst one may hesitate over some of Brand's deductions, there can be little doubt that many of these traditions go right back to pagan times. For example, the 'spring revival' theme, already described as being linked with the remaining sword dances, is clearly a continuation of very old fertility rites. The harvest festival, whilst an accepted part of the Christian Year, doubtless also existed before Christianity. The Kern Baby may now exist only in elderly recollections, but a good example was photographed early this century (Plate 139) at Whalton, a little village south-west of Morpeth. Of such things Hutchinson, in his *History of Northumberland* wrote 'I have seen . . . an Image apparelled in great finery, crowned with flowers, a sheaf of corn placed under her arm, and a scythe in her hand, carried out of the village in the morning of the conclusive reaping day, with musick and much clamour of the reapers, into the field where it stands fixed on a pole all day, and when the reaping is done, is brought home in like manner. This they call the Harvest Queen.' And to all this John Brand in 1795 added: 'An old woman . . . at a Village in Northumberland, informed me that, not half a century ago, they used every where to dress up something, similar to the figure last described, at the end of the Harvest, which was called a Harvest Doll or Kern Baby.'

It is hardly surprising that the three great human experiences, birth, marriage and death, should have retained their associated traditions longer than other activities, and many customs are still remembered, though their origins have long been forgotten. Today, for example, a christening always calls for a present and this might still be a silver mug; at very least it is a welcoming card! But not so long ago, when the baby was carried out to be seen by the neighbours it would be given a little bundle to bring good luck. In south-east Northumberland this was called an *Ammiss* bundle (probably a word derived from 'alms') which contained such 'lucky' things as salt, a 6d. (or any sort of silver coin), a candle and perhaps an egg. Salt has a lucky connotation and even today many people will still throw it over their left shoulder, to fend off the devil, if they have accidentally spilt some. A match or a candle would promise a light to help the baby's way through life and the egg represented the source of all life.

As the baby was carried to church for christening (though some say, as it was brought out of church after christening), a present was given to the first person—of the opposite sex—who met the party. This present contained cake and a silver sixpence. Norman Cowan of Newcastle remembers: 'We lived in a close-knit community of up and down flats in a long terrace . . . we soon knew when a baby was born. If a girl, all the boys were on the alert for christening day . . . I slipped out of the back door and rounded the block of flats to meet the christening party . . . The well-to-do families (earning about 25s. to 30s. a week) would have put into the parcel a piece of spice loaf, a silver sixpence and a piece of cheese. Other families would not be able to afford spice loaf and so the parcel contained a tea-cake, spread with "marg" and a tiny silver three-penny piece.'

Sometimes the word 'Ammiss' has been rationalised to 'Almonds' and sometimes it has been known simply as 'The Luck'. It has been recorded from Weardale, Wensleydale, several parts of County Durham and Northumberland. Mrs Boyd of Gateshead remembers being terrified as a girl of six when she was presented with a mysterious parcel by a complete stranger with words which sounded to her like: 'Here you are lassie, here's the baby's arms!' She thought she had been given a chopped-up baby.

Although we have all heard of a baby being born 'with a silver spoon in its mouth', it is nevertheless true that a baby may occasionally be born with a caul over its head. This is a tiny piece of the membane in which the baby was held before it was born. A baby born in a caul was supposed to be specially lucky and it would never die of drowning. The caul itself was considered to be capable of preventing drowning and hence in great demand with sailors. Frank Carlson of South Shields recalls: 'My father, who went to sea . . . always carried my caul with him. The crew on every ship on which he sailed had the greatest confidence in the caul . . . No ship in which he sailed had any major trouble even though he spent the 1914–1918 War in an ammunition carrier. He refused offers of over £100 for the caul.'

Before leaving the customs linked with birth, one may mention the belief that a baby should be taken upwards, or lifted upwards, before it was taken outdoors for the first time. Mrs Isabel Dean of Stocksfield said: 'Before a baby was taken outdoors for the first time it had to go "up" before going down the outside step or steps. So the baby was carried up one or two steps. If the house had no indoor staircase the carrier of the child stepped up on to a cracket', and Mrs Ena Joplin of Heaton recollects: 'When taking the baby into a friend's house, one chose one with stairs and the friend carried the infant upstairs at once, so he would always "go up in the world!"'

If customs are still remembered when there is a birth, how much more so when it comes to a wedding. The bride should wear 'something old, something new, something borrowed and something blue', and one wonders how many brides still keep this alive. A lady from Choppington recollects a little jingle:

'Married in White, you'll marry alright
Married in Blue, your love will be true
Married in Yellow, you'll be ashamed of your fellow
Married in Grey, you'll rue the day
Married in Red, you'll wish you were dead
Married in Black, you'll wish you were back
Married in Green, you'll not wish to be seen!'

And one particularly northern custom, still carried on, is that of throwing down pennies after the ceremony for the children who gathered round. 'Hoy a penny oot', was the cry. 'When I was young' recollects Mrs Lockey of Ormesby, 'we would gather at the bride's house, and when she returned to change, the bride-groom opened the bedroom window to throw pennies down to us. By the way, these pennies had been heated in a frying pan and were thrown down to us HOT! What a scramble!'

A variation on this was for the church gate to be locked until the bridegroom paid a 'toll' and Mrs Cooke of Hartlepool remembers this happening when she was married at Hart only a few years ago: 'The gates were tied with string and we couldn't get out until my husband threw out some change.' Apparently a custom which still prevails at the little fishing village of Boulmer is for five or six of the fishermen to gather beside the bride's home before she leaves for church. As she leaves, they fire a salvo of guns over the car.

Though customs have probably remained associated with marriage, those relating to death seem to have mostly disappeared, along with the Victorian elaborations of mourning. Even the simple courtesies are being lost. 'When any funeral passed, when I was young' recollects Miss Armstrong of Heaton, 'a woman would stand with bowed head and a man would doff his hat or cap until it passed. Now a funeral has passed before anyone realises that it *is* a funeral.' Miss Stordy of Newcastle has a childhood memory: 'When I was a small girl, the bellman where I lived used to go round the town at night bidding or inviting people to the funerals of the poorer people. He would ring his bell three times, then announce the funeral, then ring his bell again. I remember that I used to cover my head with the bed-clothes: in the dark it sounded so eerie.' Mrs Joyce Sloan of Low Fell remembers the very phrase: 'Your presence is requested at so-and-so's funeral tomorrow. Lift at ten, bury at half-past'.

The humour of the northerner is often difficult for a southerner to appreciate, and not surprisingly therefore, a joke associated with death can seem very 'sick': 'Dorfie Broon had been killed doon the pit and his marra had been told to break the news gently to his wife. So off he gans to Thord Raa and knocks at the door. When Mrs Broon answered, he asked "Dis the widder Broon live heor?" "No" says the woman. "Well she dis noo" says Geordie'. (This is a story recollected by Mrs Freda Brown of East Boldon.)

But to move to a more cheerful note, one may call to mind that the northerner is quite capable of turning the joke against himself, and here at least is a habit which is still strong. The following was heard in Morpeth Market Place around 1930, by Mr Taylor of Middlesbrough, who says that he really heard it:

Tom: 'Hear ye've got a cooncil hoose, Jake?'
Jake: 'Aye, Tom; at Stobhill'
Tom: 'Hev ye got a lend of a cart?'
Jake: 'What for?'
Tom: 'Te tak yor forniture te Stobhill'
Jake: 'Divvent be se daft, Tom. Aal aa need is a hay fork!'

And finally, since we seem to have got onto a joke-telling session, if old oft-repeated jokes can be accepted as part of our continuing lore, one may be forgiven for ending this book with a charmingly naive little story. One should add that to modern ears jokes of fifty and more years ago may seem very unsophisticated and here is such a one, recalled by Mr Blewitt of Darlington. In it reference is made to an iron hoop which children *booled* or rolled along the ground, whilst running alongside it.

'This is the story of a man who only had 1s. 6d. in his pocket and went to buy a car. Well the sympathetic salesman sent him to a cycle shop to buy a bike. Same again, the man there sent him to a toy department to buy a scooter. No luck again, but the astute salesman sold him a booler.

Well he was very happy with this and off he went round the streets and out of town, 'cos it was a nice day for a run. Twenty-five miles on he was very thirsty, so he parked his booler outside a pub while he went in for some refreshment.

When he came out somebody had pinched his booler so back he went inside to complain to the inn-keeper. To placate him the inn-keeper offered to reimburse him, to which he replied:—

"That's alright for you but how the hell am I going to get back home?" '

Some books about North-East England

On such a vast subject, capable of being studied in great depth or treated in the most casual way, it is difficult to choose a reasonable selection of recent and generally readable books or booklets. This selection is therefore a rather personal one.

To begin with the geology of the region, from which it has all developed, one might mention two general and none-too-technical books *Geology and Scenery in England & Wales* by A. E. Trueman (1949), and *Britain's Structure & Scenery* by L. Dudley Stamp (1946). These are not only easily understood but quite enjoyable. A very helpful booklet particularly for teachers is *Geographical Field Studies in the Durham Area* published in 1967 by the University of Durham Institute of Education. Of course if one is seeking specific information on the geology of the region *The Geology of Northern England,* HMSO 1971 is essential. On the wider subject of man-made landscape, one cannot do better than read *The Northumberland Landscape* by Robert Newton (1972) and another readable and informative geographical book is *North England* by A. E. Smailes (1960).

To learn something of the early northern settlers one has to read various archaeological and historical booklets and a fine series is that published by Frank Graham of Newcastle, with such titles as *Castles of the Northumbrian Coast, Those Delavals* and *Anglo-Saxon Northumbria.* There are very useful articles on a whole range of topics in *Durham County & City with Teesside* published by the British Association for the Advancement of Science in 1970. Topics of articles in this volume include vegetational history, the archaeology of several periods, rural settlement, place-names, population growth, genetic characteristics and recent aspects of planning.

Little in the way of general books has been written on upland agriculture in the North-East, but Dales lead-mining is well described in *The History of Lead Mining in the North East* by Les Turnbull (1975). Two other informative, though more specialised, books are *A History of Lead Mining in the Pennines* by Raistrick and Jennings (1965) and *The Lead Miners of the Northern Pennines* by C. J. Hunt (1970).

The subject of vernacular building is now being written about much more than it was a few years ago and a good general introduction to the subject is *Illustrated Handbook of Vernacular Architecture* by R. W. Brunskill (1971). A specialised but richly detailed and well-illustrated book is *Shielings and Bastles* (1970) an HMSO publication on the border counties of Cumberland and Northumberland.

On such lowland matters as 'green villages', nothing has yet been written for the general reader, though there is an excellent article by Brian Roberts in the British Association volume already mentioned.

Of maritime matters, one should mention David Dougan's *History of North-East Shipbuilding* (1968), and a vivid description of the problems of that industry in the North-East in the 20s is to be found in *Industrial Tyneside: A Social Survey* by Henry Mess (1928).

This leads to one of the north's chief industries, coal mining and here a general book is Frank Atkinson's *The Great Northern Coalfield, 1700–1900* (1966 and 1968). *Mostly Mining* by William Moyes (1969) is a lively study of the development of Easington Rural District.

On the general subject of the industrial development of the region one cannot do better than quote a broad-based booklet by David Rowe: *The Economy of the North East in the Nineteenth Century: A Survey* (1973). And on such important topics as railways, there is a virtual plethora of books. The basis of many is W. W. Tomlinson's *North Eastern Railway: Its Rise and Development,* published in 1914 and re-issued in 1967. Ken Hoole's *Railways of North East England* (1965) is still an authoritative work. On the wider subject of industrial archaeology, there are Frank Atkinson's *Industrial Archaeology of North East England* (1974) in two volumes and booklet *Top Ten Industrial Archaeological Sites in North East England* (1971). Two fascinating booklets, each titled *Eyewitness,* have been compiled by Edwin Miller and published by the Sunderland College of Education, one with the sub-title *The Industrial Revolution in the North East* (1967) and the other *The North East in the early Nineteenth Century* (1968).

As to the chief city of the North-East, there are many books one could mention, a good one on which to begin being *Newcastle upon Tyne: Its Growth & Achievement* by S. Middlebrook (1950). The work of Grainger, Dobson and Clayton has never been better described than in *Tyneside Classical* by Lyall Wilkes and Gordon Dodds (1964) and more about other buildings in the city is to be seen and read about in *Historic Architecture of Newcastle upon Tyne* by Bruce Allsopp (1967). *Kiddar's Luck* (first published in 1951, and reprinted in 1975), by Jack Common, is an autobiographical novel by one of Tyneside's able writers. It includes many lively descriptions of the city in the early years of this century. And of course other novelists of the region such as Catherine Cookson and Sid Chaplin have poured much of their northern lives into their novels.

As to the people themselves, the dialect, their songs and their traditions, an amusing beginning point (if not taken too seriously) might be *Larn Yersel' Geordie* by Scott Dobson, first published in 1969, but run into many reprints and other editions since then. On a more serious note, *A Word Geography of England* by Orton and Wright (1975) is a tremendous source of dialectal information and the first notation of the northern sword dances is in a booklet by Cecil Sharp *The Sword Dancers of Northern England,* published in three parts around 1912. The music of the region is now appearing in a remarkable range of gramophone records: its songs, ballads and pipe-music.

Finally, a most attractive publication is *The Durham Book* (1973) published by Frank Graham for Durham County Council and prepared by Richard Atkinson, County Planning Officer.

Index